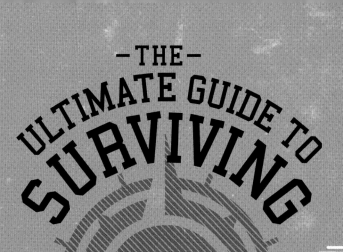

# —THE—
# ULTIMATE GUIDE TO
# SURVIVING
# IN THE
# WILD

## CLIVE GIFFORD

Quarto is the authority on a wide range of topics.

Quarto educates, entertains and enriches the lives of our readers—enthusiasts and lovers of hands-on living.

www.quartoknows.com

© 2018 Quarto Publishing plc

Author: Clive Gifford
Designed and edited by Tall Tree Ltd

This edition first published in 2018
by QEB Publishing,
an imprint of The Quarto Group.
6 Orchard Road
Suite 100
Lake Forest, CA 92630
T: +1 949 380 7510
F: +1 949 380 7575
www.QuartoKnows.com

A CIP record for this book is available from the Library of Congress.

ISBN: 978-1-78603-360-4

Manufactured in Dongguan, China
TL112018

9 8 7 6 5 4 3 2 1

MIX
Paper from responsible sources
FSC® C104723
www.fsc.org

**Acknowledgements**
The publisher thanks the following agencies for their kind permission to use their images.

Key: fc= front cover, t=top, b=bottom, l=left, r=right

**Alamy**
86 © Finnbarr Webster Editorial

**Dreamstime**
10b © Ekaterina Pokrovsky, 11t © Shannon Fagan, 11b © Pavel Losevsky, 12 © Irimaxim, 13t © Iakov Filimonov, 13b © Ferdericb, 14b © Aarstudio, 15tr © Vaeenma, 15tl © Xbrchx, 15b © Jarosław Janczuk, 16 © Ecophoto, 17 © Natallia Yaumenenka, 18 © Hecke01, 19tl © Daniel Boiteau, 19tr © Flavijus, 19b © Anthony Hathaway, 20 © Kkistl01, 21tr © Guy Sagi, 21b © Palex66, 25t © Fotoeye75, 26 © Robert Apple, 27bl © Björn Wylezich, 33tr © Jason Ondreicka, 34 © Warrengoldswain, 35tr © Lukaves, 36 © Filipe Frazao, 37 © Wrangel, 41c © Michael Lynch, 43c © Anthony Hathaway, 45b © Dennis Jacobsen, 47 © VOLODYMYR SERGEIEV, 51tl © Nordroden, 51b © Dalia Kvedaraite, 53t © Maximka87, 54 © Volodymyr Shevchuk, 55t © Nikita Buida, 55b © Erectus, 56 © Galyna Andrushko, 57t © Dani3315, 57b © Dmytro Pylypenko, 58 © Roman Lysogor, 59tr © Uatp1, 60 © Oliver1803, 61 © Nick Everett, 65t © Shuo Wang, 66 © Dimarik16, 71 © Andrew Kazmierski, 73c © Meisterphotos, 75 © Christopher Meder, 75c © Setik0, 76 © Jzehnder1, 77b © Bevanward, 79t © Fritz Hiersche, 79b © Lukas Blazek, 80 © Michael Wood, 81 © Ian Fish, 84 © Sergey Kelin, 92–93 © Andrey Shupilo, 93tr © Kozzi2, 93c © Mikhail Dudarev

**Shutterstock.com**
fc © Malashkos, 1 © MP cz, 1 © Tyler Olson, 4 © Kletr, 4–5 & 8–9 © Piotr Grzymkowski, 5t © Alizada Studios, 5b © Alexander Chlum, 6–7 © lzf, 8t © Panaponera, 9b © reptiles4all, 21tl © Asmiana, 22 © Krishna.Wu, 23 © sirtravelalot, 24 © Ondra Vacek, 25b © Brian Lasenby, 27t © K.Sorokin, 27tl & cr & br © Maksim Shmeljov, 27cl © Pinglabel, 28 © VladFotoMag, 29tl © lera_virskaya, 29tr © Astrid Hill, 29cl © Wollertz, 29cr © Elvan, 29br © Cannon Colegrove, 30 © lzf, 31bl & br © Jannarong, 32 © Scott E Read, 33tl © creativex, 33cl © Karel Bartik, 33cl © Geoffrey Kuchera, 33cr © PhotoTrippingAmerica, 33cr © Mircea Costina, 35b © Tom Reichner, 38 © Rawpixel.com, 39 © Patrick K. Campbell, 40 © nechaevkon, 41t © Lana Kray, 41b © Ryan M. Bolton, 42 © guentermanaus, 43tl © Erik Klietsch, 44 © Jess Kraft, 45t © JM-Design, 46 © Ammit Jack, 48c © Fridi, 49b © Doptis, 50b © everst, 51tr © Avatar_023, 52 © All-stock-photos, 53c © Dinga, 59tl © Lisa Parsons, 62 © Helen Hotson, 63tl © Amanda Nicholls, 63cr © Keat Eung, 64 © M600i, 65b © cbpix, 67t © Natalia Siiatovskaia, 67c © ATK WORK, 68 © Deatonphotos, 70 © Tero Hakala, 72 © Pics by Nick, 73t © oneinchpunch, 77t © Sundays Photography, 78 © amophoto_au, 81b © J.A. Dunbar, 81b © Alizada Studios, 81b © ChameleonsEye, 82 © irabel8, 83 © Matt9122, 85br © Olesia Bilkei, 85bl © Photobank gallery, 87br © maikbrand, 87c © Dewald Kirsten, 87bl © IVANNE, 88 © Sergey Nivens, 89bl © Graham D Elliott, 89br © GUDKOV ANDREY, 90 © divedog, 91br © Rich Carey, 93tr © Ryan Lewandowski, 96 © Sanchik

**Public Domain**
69b © Brocken Inaglory, 75t © Sputnikcccp, 75b © Greg Hume

# -THE-
## ULTIMATE GUIDE TO
## SURVIVING
## IN THE
## WILD

QEB

# CONTENTS

# INTRODUCTION

Whether you're marooned on a desert island, lost near the South Pole, or trapped alone in the Rocky Mountains, this book offers expert survival tips and facts that will help keep you safe, and improve your chances of survival in the wild. Get acquainted with wild creatures, learn how to get spotted and rescued in the wilderness, and discover extraordinary tales of real life survivors who showed bravery and ingenuity to get out of alarming situations.

## TAKE CARE!

Take care wherever you see this sign. Never undertake any of the tips next to one of these symbols unless you are accompanied by an experienced and qualified survival expert!

Exploring Earth's wildernesses can be fun and exhilarating, but never underestimate how dangerous they can be!

# LOST IN THE SAHARA DESERT

The Sahara Desert is the world's biggest hot, dry desert, stretching all the way across North Africa. It's a SERIOUSLY scary place to get lost. Large areas of this deadly desert are nothing more than roasting hot sand dunes, rocks, and pebbles. But in some places, there are scrubby plants, flowers, a few trees, and oases, where natural fresh springs flow out of the ground.

MEDITERRANEAN SEA

SAHARA DESERT

You are here!

N
W    E
S

AFRICA

ATLANTIC OCEAN

## Sahara Desert fact file
**Area:**
3,550,000 square miles (9,200,000 km²)—almost as big as the USA!
**Maximum temperature:**
136.4°F (58°C)
**Average rainfall:**
3 inches (7.5 cm) per year

So…how on earth do you get lost in the Sahara Desert? Sometimes people drive into the desert, then get cut off by a sandstorm, or stuck in the middle of nowhere when their car breaks down. Planes have crashed in the desert, and anyone who escapes alive is left to face the elements. Some people run into trouble while trekking across the desert on foot—a pretty dangerous thing to try.

## WHAT TO DO FIRST

If you don't act fast, you'll soon succumb to the Sahara's super-harsh conditions. The main dangers you face are:

- Sweltering heat
- Dazzling, burning sun
- Lack of water
- Freezing cold temperatures at night
- Sandstorms (if you're unlucky)
- Deadly animals (more on them later!)

### Keep cool

If you need to move, look to travel early in the morning or late in the evening to avoid the sun's full glare. Stay in the shade as much as possible, either in the shadow of a car or plane, behind rocks, or in a cave.

### Stay with your vehicle

If you have a vehicle such as a car or plane, stay close to it, as a large object like this will help rescuers to spot you. But don't sit inside it, as it may get dangerously hot.

### Drink water

If you have a water supply, keep sipping it. DON'T ration it or save it. Don't leave lids off bottles, as the water will evaporate.

### Beware mirages

These illusions, caused by the heat, can make sand appear as a shimmering pool of water ahead.

## CREATURE FEATURE: SAW-SCALED VIPER

This snake, also called the carpet viper, is perfectly camouflaged, and very small—only 12–24 inches (30–60 cm) long. If you step on one, it won't hesitate to strike and bite you with its poison-filled fangs. To avoid it, listen for the shaking, scraping warning sound it makes by rubbing its scales together.

# WATER WORKS

Deserts are defined as regions which receive less than 1 inch (250 mm) of rainfall a year. Much of the Sahara receives less than half of that. With fierce heat, and your body potentially losing as much as a quart (950 ml) of sweat an hour, water is your number one priority. You can survive for only a handful of days without water. So, seek out a supply before you do anything else.

The landscape around you may appear dusty and dry, but water can lurk beneath or just out of view. Here's where you might find water...

## Base of slopes and cliffs

A good site for a potential pool, spring, or underground water source. Choose north-facing slopes which are in shade for most of the hottest part of the day.

## Birds

Most creatures don't live far from water. Bees, for example, fly no more than 2–2.5 miles (3–4 km) away from a regular water source. Low-flying birds may be full of water they've just drunk, so note their direction.

## Wadis

A wadi is a valley or gulley, usually formed by a river which has dried up. Head to the outside bend of a dry river bed and dig down.

## Plants

A large clump of bushes and other plants, especially ones with broad, green leaves, can indicate moisture below ground.

# GET PRACTICAL:
## DIG FOR VICTORY

When you think you've found a source of water, start to dig.

**1.** Do your digging in the very early morning when groundwater is usually nearest the surface.

**2.** Dig down 12 inches (30 cm) and if the ground feels sticky or wet, keep on digging. If it's still dry, save your energy and pick a target elsewhere.

**3.** A pool of water may form at the bottom of your hole. If the water's hard to reach, use a cloth or spare t-shirt to soak it up then squeeze it out into a container right away before it can evaporate.

# REAL-LIFE SURVIVORS

In December 1935, Antoine de Saint-Exupéry and Andre Prévot crashed their plane in the Sahara. They salvaged a flask of coffee, chocolate, grapes, and two oranges, and even licked dew off the wings of their wrecked plane. However, after two days, the pair were suffering from dehydration, which caused confusion and hallucinations. They were saved just in the nick of time by a Bedouin traveler. Another day or two would have seen them perish.

## A wet welcome

An oasis is a place in the desert where underground water from a spring or river reaches the surface. Often surrounded by trees, an isolated oasis can attract animal life from long distances.

IF YOU'RE STUCK IN THE DESERT FOR DAYS, CONSIDER MAKING A SOLAR STILL (SEE P89).

# HOT STUFF!

Have we mentioned that the Sahara can be hot, hot, hot? Temperatures average over 86°F (30°C) in most parts, and in the height of summer can soar above 113°F (45°C).

 Look to stay cool at all times by following these tips.

## Wear lightweight clothes

Clothes should be light in weight and color and loose fitting, so that a layer of air billows between the clothes and your body, helping to keep you cool. Make sure your arms and legs are completely covered to protect against sunburn.

## Use sunglasses

These help cut down the glare from the harsh sunlight. If you find the sun's glare particularly fierce, use colored tape over your glasses to form long, narrow slits to peer through.

## Close your mouth

Breathe through your nose to stop your mouth and throat from drying up. Your nostrils also contain hairs and mucus to help filter out dust from the air.

## Put on a hat

Wear a wide-brimmed hat at all times to shield you from the sun. If you only have a baseball cap, jam it on over the top of a cloth to protect your neck and the back of your head. If you have plenty of water, wet the cloth before you put it on. As it dries out, the evaporating water will cool your head and neck.

# CREATURE FEATURE:
## HARDY DORCAS GAZELLE

The dorcas gazelle is a small antelope found throughout the Sahara. Standing 22–26 inches (55–65 cm) high at the shoulder, they are well-adapted to life in the desert. They can go without drinking water for months at a time. Instead, they get their moisture from leaves, fruits, and plant stems. When temperatures are high, copy their behavior by staying inactive during the heat of the day and being active at night when it is cooler.

## Sunstroke

Sunstroke occurs when your body has a temperature above 104°F (40°C) and overheats. It can lead to dizziness, headaches, vomiting, breathing difficulties, and fainting. Get into shade and lie down. Use wet cloths to cool your face and neck.

## Desert headwear

Saharan desert peoples have worn headscarves for centuries. The Tuareg's *tagelmust* is a 20-foot- (6-m-) long piece of wound cloth that covers their entire face, leaving a gap for the eyes and nose. Make a simple version by winding a 10 to 13-foot- (3–4-m-) long piece of cloth around your head and face with the end tucked in.

# DESERT FOOD

Food gives you the energy and nutrients your body needs to grow and repair itself. Unlike water, you can survive without food for many days. Let's think about what kinds of foods you might find in the desert.

If you find yourself in the Sahara due to a plane or vehicle crash, you may come across an abandoned camp or stray pack animal carrying supplies. Which foods should you go for?

## Survival rations

If you have lots of water, it can be used to rehydrate nutritious dried meals in pouches to sustain you.

## Canned goods

Choose cans that contain non-salty liquid which you can drink, as well as eating the contents. No can opener? Use a sharp rock to puncture holes in the top of the can so you can get at its contents. Alternatively, wear away the top lip of the can by rubbing it vigorously on a flat, rocky area. Then, squeeze the can's sides hard to try to pop the lid open.

## Fruit and veggies

Moist, fresh fruit and veggies are a good choice. Bananas, avocados, and passion fruit are rich in carbohydrates and minerals, such as potassium, which is lost during heavy sweating.

## High energy

Hard candies, isotonic sports drink tablets, and trail snacks, such as granola bars, dried fruits, nuts, seeds, and cookies can provide a quick energy boost.

# STAYING ALIVE:
## EDIBLE PLANTS

Rough grasses and scrubby bushes are common vegetation in the desert, but there are plants which can offer you sustenance.

### 1. Acacia tree
The 20–33 foot (6–10 m) tall, thorny acacia tree has yellow flowers, young leaves, and pod seeds, which are all edible.

### 2. Fig tree
Fig trees are found in oases and produce large numbers of tasty fig fruits (below). The entire fruit, including the skin, can be eaten.

### 3. Date palm (right)
Dates are highly nutritious and calorific—as much as 70 calories per fruit. Most palm groves in the Sahara are tended by people —increasing your chances of rescue.

### 4. Wild desert gourd
Also known as the bitter cucumber, this plant produces bitter-tasting fruit from sprawling vines. Eat the flowers and chew on the juicy stem tips to obtain water but avoid eating the fruit, which can give you painful stomach cramps.

# CREATURE FEATURE:
## OSTRICH ALERT

An ostrich egg could be a valuable treat. A single egg can make an omelet the size of 20 chicken eggs. However, beware, ostriches are the largest living bird and can deliver dangerous blows with their powerful legs. Keep at least 150 paces away, as you cannot outrun an ostrich. Their top sprinting speed is over 37 mph (60 km/h).

# STORMS OF SAND

Giant clouds of sand and dust sometimes sweep across the Sahara. Propelled by violent winds, these sandstorms can blast and scour everything in their path, causing injury, as well as burying or suffocating living things.

If a sandstorm appears to be heading your way, don't panic. Follow these tips and you should be able to ride out the storm.

## Seek shelter

You can rarely outrun a sandstorm. Instead, focus on finding a suitable place for shelter, such as behind a large boulder or rocky outcrop. Don't head into a low, hollow area as it might get buried.

## Hunker down

Get into position and use your backpack or bag to protect your head. Place the crook of your arm over your eyes and bow your head a little.

## Stay still

With limited visibility and sand lashing your body, moving during a sandstorm can be deadly. Be patient and wait out the storm.

## Protect your face

Wear a *tagelmust* (see p13) or headscarf to help stop sand, dust, and grit from pummeling your face. Alternatively, wet a cloth or spare t-shirt and wrap it around your nose and mouth to protect your airways. If you have any vaseline, apply a little to the inside of your nostrils.

# CREATURE FEATURE:
## ULTIMATE SAHARA SURVIVOR

These "ships of the desert" are well adapted to life in the Sahara. Their broad feet enable them to walk on soft sand and their large humps store fat so they can last long periods without food.
To protect their eyes, they have a third eyelid, and, during a sandstorm, they can close their nostrils. Their ears are also lined with fur to prevent sand from getting in.

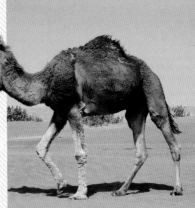

# REAL-LIFE SURVIVOR

In 1994, 39-year-old Italian policeman Mauro Prosperi got lost while running a long-distance Sahara race. Caught in a violent sandstorm, he ended up heading over 125 miles (200 km) in the wrong direction, leaving Morocco and entering Algeria.

Totally alone, Mauro survived ten days in the harsh desert. He sheltered in a marabout (see p19), used his own urine to rehydrate his dried food, and caught and ate lizards, snakes, and even bats. On the eighth day, Mauro found a small oasis with water. He also spotted goats in the distance which gave him hope of finding people. By the time he found a camp of Berber people, he had lost 35 pounds (16 kg) and was suffering from liver damage. It took almost two years to recover fully, yet astonishingly, he returned to race across the desert in 1998.

"I WAS SWALLOWED BY A YELLOW WALL OF SAND.
I WAS BLINDED, I COULDN'T BREATHE. THE SAND WHIPPED MY
FACE—IT WAS LIKE A STORM OF NEEDLES."

# STAY OR GO?

It's a tough call. You may have good shelter or be near a crashed vehicle with lots of water and other supplies. In these cases, you might choose to stay and signal for rescue (see p21). But if you can spot signs of other people, better shelter, or an oasis in the distance, you may choose to move.

 If you decide to make a move, what else should you consider?

 ## Walk in boots

The Sahara is more than 16 times bigger than the whole of France, but only around a fifth of it is made up of sand dunes. The rest is rocky pavements, gravel plains, and mountains. So go for stout and strong walking boots that will let you cover all terrains.

 ## Stay on track

If you are on soft sand, don't expect your progress to be fast. If possible, trek along rocky pavements or walk in tracks made by other people or creatures who have already pressed the sand down.

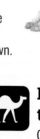

 ## Use high ground

Reaching the top of a ridge or rocky plateau can give you a good vantage point to spot an oasis or a town. At other times, keep cool by walking at its base, traveling in shade cast by the higher ground.

## Head for the camels

Convoys of camels known as caravans or trains are still used by desert people to carry goods. A camel train may even carry tourists. If you see camels, wave your arms and shout for help.

# SIGNS OF LIFE:
## DESERT LANDMARKS

Keep an eye out for landmarks to stay on track. There may also be manmade signs of life that will give you clues along the way.

### 1. Marabouts (left)
These are religious shrines used by Muslim travelers in the desert. They can provide shelter out of the sun. One saved Mauro Prosperi's life (see p17).

### 2. Ghost towns
These are villages and camps that have been abandoned but their buildings remain. They can provide shade as well as useful tools and materials.

### 3. Well, well, WELL!
Wells, sometimes known as ganats, can be found in the desert. Abandoned settlements around mines may also contain deep wells.

# CREATURE FEATURE:
## STRIPED HYENA

Hyenas mostly live in the dry grassy plains south of the Sahara, but some venture into the more mountainous parts of the desert. These scavengers hunt mostly at night, often alone or in small numbers. They have been known to attack humans, particularly those sleeping rough. Keep a fire going to keep them at bay.

USE THE STARS AT NIGHT TO NAVIGATE AND FIND NORTH (SEE P31).

# SLEEP AND SIGNALING

You have water, food, and—perhaps—a plan, but what do you do when you need to rest? Keep an eye out on your desert trek for suitable locations to sleep safely and think carefully about where and how you can signal for help.

 You still need to keep your wits about you if you stop to rest or sleep. Here's what you need to look out for...

## Beat it!

Before you lie down to rest, stamp your feet and beat the ground with sticks. This helps alert any scorpions or snakes sheltering nearby, so they can scuttle and slither off.

## Night shivers

Temperatures in the Sahara can plummet to near freezing at night. Layer clothes and wear a hat to keep heat in. A fire made from dry tree wood enclosed in a ring of stones can help keep you warm.

## Shaded site

During the day, pick a place to rest that gives you significant shade, such as a rocky outcrop or a cave. At night, use a flashlight or other light source, and make noise or throw stones inside a cave before entering, to flush out any creatures.

# GET PRACTICAL:
# DESERT RESCUE!

The Sahara can feel featureless but it could make you more visible and help you attract attention from planes, helicopters, distant settlements, or other travelers.

### 1. Mirror, mirror
A mirror can reflect rays over large distances. If you don't have one, improvise with a shiny surface, such as a metal belt buckle. Angle it so you reflect the sun in the direction you want to signal.

### 2. Distress signal
Make a fire on the top of a rocky ridge so that it can be seen over many miles. Building three fires 30–60 feet (9–18 m) apart in a triangle pattern is an internationally-recognized distress signal.

# CREATURE FEATURE:
# SCORPION ALERT!

Some 30 species of scorpion are found in the Sahara. They gain much of their moisture from their prey and when food is scarce, they can slow their bodies down to conserve energy. Some species have powerful venom, which they apply using the stinger on the end of their tail. The deathstalker scorpion is one of the desert's deadliest. It averages around $2\frac{1}{8}$ to $2\frac{3}{8}$ inches (55–60 mm) long and is often straw-colored. Its venom can kill small children and weak or ill adults.

# MISSING IN THE ROCKIES

The Rockies are a series of mountain ranges that run 2,860 miles (4,600 km) in western North America, from northern British Columbia to New Mexico. The landscape varies from thick forests, rushing streams, and lakes, to meadows and rugged wilderness. In such a diverse region, the climate varies too. It can range from scorching hot 86°F+ (30°C+) summers in southern lowland areas to sub-zero conditions in the mountains. It's breathtakingly beautiful, but if you're stranded alone and unprepared, can also be dangerous.

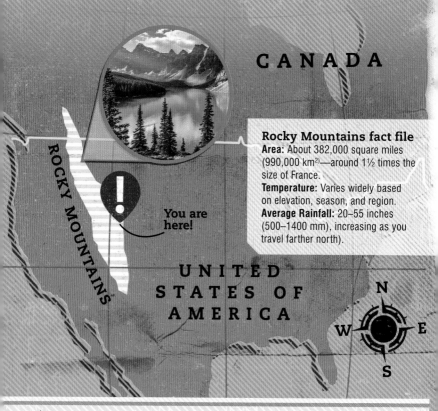

CANADA

ROCKY MOUNTAINS

**You are here!**

### Rocky Mountains fact file
**Area:** About 382,000 square miles (990,000 km²)—around 1½ times the size of France.
**Temperature:** Varies widely based on elevation, season, and region.
**Average Rainfall:** 20–55 inches (500–1400 mm), increasing as you travel farther north).

UNITED STATES OF AMERICA

N
W    E
S

So how did you end up on your own in the Rockies—North America's biggest and deadliest mountain range? You might have been the victim of a hike that went wrong, wandered off during a school expedition or been in a car that broke down, leaving you stranded.

## WHAT TO DO FIRST

Separated from others by large areas of rugged terrain and wilderness, your main dangers are:

- Intense cold in some regions
- Major weather changes and temperature swings
- Storms, snow, and lightning

- Rock falls and landslides
- Lack of water and food
- Tough terrain to cross and climb
- Animal attacks

### Assess the weather

Depending on conditions, you might need to get out of the scorching sun, shelter from oncoming storms, or find warmth before nightfall.

### Look for people

Recall your journey. Did you see any park ranger huts, roads, hikers, or camps earlier? Are there other people nearby?

### Look for water

Seek out clean, fresh water to drink and fill water bottles. Search your camp or vehicle for water and empty containers, and listen for gurgling streams, brooks or rushing rivers close by.

### Dial 911

You may not have the Internet, but you might be able to call up the GPS feature on your smartphone for location coordinates. If you have a signal, dial 911—the emergency number in Canada and the USA.

## CREATURE FEATURE: MOUNTAIN LION

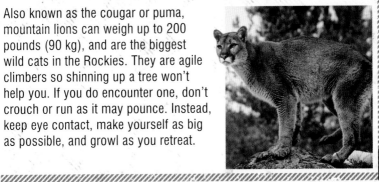

Also known as the cougar or puma, mountain lions can weigh up to 200 pounds (90 kg), and are the biggest wild cats in the Rockies. They are agile climbers so shinning up a tree won't help you. If you do encounter one, don't crouch or run as it may pounce. Instead, keep eye contact, make yourself as big as possible, and growl as you retreat.

# UP HIGH

The Rockies contain more than 300 peaks that reach nearly 13,000 feet (4,000 m) high and large stretches of land above 10,000 feet (3,000 m). At these heights, sunburn is a real threat even if the temperature is cool or cold, so wear sunscreen. The weather can change suddenly, with temperatures plummeting at nightfall.

If you're on your own in the mountains, how do you protect yourself from the elements and find shelter?

## Layers

Wear plenty of layers and try to keep dry. In the cold, as much as half of all heat loss comes from a bare head, so wear a warm hat.

## Insulation

If resting, use branches, moss, bracken, and leaves to build a platform an inch or two off the ground to insulate you against the cold earth.

## Caves and overhangs

Look for a natural shelter such as a cave or a small rocky overhang which you can cover with branches. Don't just wander straight into a cave. Before you enter, check near the entrance for food debris, animal droppings, fur, or anything that shows an animal might be living there.

## Hypothermia

This occurs when your body temperature falls below 95°F (35°C). Signs include uncontrollable shivering and numb skin, often followed by confusion, clumsiness, and a lack of energy. Get warm—climb into your sleeping bag and consume hot drinks.

## Natural sunscreen

If you're out of sunscreen, look for quaking aspen trees. Their leaves, and sometimes the trunk, may have a whitish powder on its surface. It can make a weak sun block with an SPF (sun protection factor) of around five.

# REAL-LIFE SURVIVOR

Ruby Stein feared the worst when she and her cat, Nikki, got stuck in her car for five days in the wintry Colorado Rockies in 2017. This 85-year-old woman used old clothes to seal up gaps in the car doors that were letting cold air in and safety-pinned clothes together to make a warm blanket. She also melted snow in an old cat food can to keep herself and her cat hydrated before being rescued by two hikers.

## CREATURE FEATURE:
# MOOSE ON THE LOOSE

Moose, the largest of all deer species, are well-equipped for the cold. They have warm fur and their large hooves spread the weight of 440–1,540 pounds (200–700 kg) over snowy or soft, muddy ground so they don't sink. They're normally placid, but can be aggressive in mating season (early autumn) and sometimes charge. Males, with their 6-½-foot- (2-m-) wide antlers, could do serious damage. Flee and get yourself behind stout, closely-packed trees to keep an angry moose at bay.

TO GAIN VITAL TIPS ON HOW TO SURVIVE AN AVALANCHE SEE P58

# KICKING UP A STORM

The Rockies' variable and changing weather can create many hazards besides extreme temperatures. Heavy rain can cause small flash floods, rock falls, or landslides, while sudden wind gusts may uproot trees or lead to falling branches. Thunderstorms can suddenly appear, complete with lashing rain, wind, and lightning strikes.

Getting hit by lightning, although very rare, can result in severe injury or death. If there's a storm, find a safe place, like a cave, to shelter in or follow these tips...

### Avoid metal

Keep away from wire fences or any other metal objects that can conduct electricity. Don't hold metal objects either.

### Crouch down

If you're out in the open, crouch low down on the balls of your feet with your heels up to reduce your contact with the ground as much as possible.

### Keep to low ground

Stay on low ground and avoid standing close to the tallest thing nearby, such as a lone tree. Water conducts electricity so avoid standing near lakes, rivers, or ponds.

### Count the seconds

Sound travels much slower than light, so there is a gap between seeing a distant lightning strike and hearing a thunderclap. Count the seconds between the two and divide by 5 to show roughly how far away lightning is from you in miles.

# Signs of a storm

Certain signs will tell you that a storm could be heading your way. These include a sudden drop in temperature and a strong change of wind direction. If your watch has a barometer, which measures air pressure, a sudden drop in air pressure can indicate a storm is coming. In addition, if you're well inland from the coast, spotting gulls and other seabirds may also be a sign of a storm on its way.

# Storm-bringers

Certain cloud formations can also signal that a big storm is coming. Spotting these clouds early may give you more time to seek shelter.

**1. Altostratus**.
Found lower in the sky than cirrus clouds, these often indicate an approaching change in the weather. They can develop into nimbostratus clouds.

**2. Nimbostratus**.
These gray, heavy clouds are often low in the sky and tend to bring continuous medium-to-heavy rain or snowfall.

**3. Cirrus**.
High level wispy or tufty clouds associated with good weather.

**4. Cumulonimbus**. These are the daddy of all storm clouds. Some are over 33,000 feet (10,000 m) high and usually have a flat top shaped like an anvil. They often produce heavy rainfall or hail, thunderstorms, and lightning.

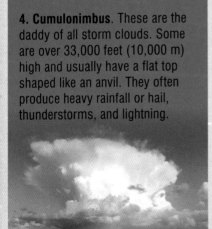

**5. Altocumulus**.
White or gray clouds that are found in rounded fluffy patches throughout the sky. If you see them on a warm morning, there is a good chance of a thunderstorm that afternoon.

# FOOD FOR THOUGHT

Spend any length of time in the wilderness and you're going to get hungry and thirsty. Fortunately, both of your needs can be met naturally. Look around and you may find a source of drinking water and plants that are safe to eat.

A fire will allow you to boil water and cook the plants you find to make them more digestible. Try one of the following fires...

## Star fire

This is an easy-to-maintain fire that is good for night time. Lay 4-8 logs in a star shape with tinder and small sticks placed in the middle. Push the logs into the middle as they burn.

## Stones and sticks

If you lack pots and pans, you can still cook. Stones can be heated on top or under a fire and used as a grill. A sharpened stick can be used to cook food over a fire. Strong, durable tree bark can make simple food containers.

## Yukon stove

A good fire if it's windy. Dig a hole in the ground and then a small tunnel to one side. Build a chimney out of stones and pack earth around the main hole and place firewood inside. Place tinder in the small tunnel and light it before pushing it into the bottom of the fire.

## Swedish log fire

If the ground is snowy or soaking wet, make a Swedish log fire (below). Try to split the top of a log into a cross shape. Pack the gaps in the top of the log with dry tinder and place a little more tinder and smaller sticks on the top. Once the log starts to burn solidly, place cooking containers on top.

# STAYING ALIVE:
## EDIBLE PLANTS

Under extreme circumstances, you may need to look for plants and fruits to eat. However, be very cautious as some plants could also make you ill (see p74).

**1. Fruits and nuts**. Look for wild strawberries, cranberries, blueberries, and redcurrants (above). Nutritious pine nuts can be found in pinyon pine trees.

**2. Leaves.** Watercress (left), alfalfa, and waterleaf can be eaten raw, as can curly dock and dandelion leaves.

**3. Flowers**. Some plants have flowers you can eat. These include dandelions and the white flowers of the low-lying candytuft plant (above).

**4. Bulbs and roots**. Yampa, wild hyacinth, and wild onions (below) have edible bulbs or tubers under the ground. Use a pointed stick to dig them out of the soil.

# CREATURE FEATURE:
## FISH FOOD

While you may prefer to catch a juicy rainbow or brown trout to eat, you are more likely to snare a mountain whitefish, which is also edible. These are typically 10–16 inches (25–40 cm) long and are found in rivers throughout the Rockies, where they feed on aquatic insects.

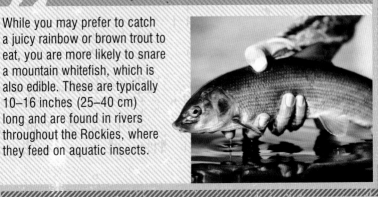

# WILDERNESS SKILLS

Certain skills and tips can help you as you travel through the Rockies, such as walking on trails that other people have used, as well as knowing how to navigate, tie useful knots, build shelters, and fashion simple tools.

 As you walk through the wilderness, you need to tread carefully to avoid any falls or injuries. Look out for the following...

 ## Dig in

When walking up steep slopes, dig your heels in to get a good grip. Try walking diagonally up and across a slope in a zig-zagging pattern. A branch can make a useful walking stick for support.

 ## Loose rocks

Concentrate on where you place your feet, especially on rocky terrain, as loose rock and stone can lead to slips, falls, and twisted joints.

 ## Moving down

When traveling down a steep slope, keep your legs slightly bent at the knee to act as a shock absorber. Take short steps and watch out for loose rocks or wet and icy patches.

# Finding your way

If you don't have a compass, you can still navigate using:

**1. The stars**. To find north at night, look for the pattern of stars called the Big Dipper or Plough. The two end stars of this formation point upward to Polaris—the pole star that appears in the sky directly above the North Pole.

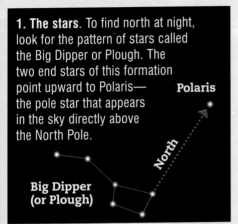

**Polaris**

**North**

**Big Dipper (or Plough)**

**2. A watch**. If you are in the Rockies and you have a watch with hands, point the hour hand at the sun. A line halfway between the hour hand and 12 o'clock gives the north-south line.

## GET PRACTICAL: GET KNOTTED!

**1. Clove hitch**. Used to tie a rope to a branch or pole. Take the rope over and under the pole, and cross the rope's end over to form an X shape. Take the rope around again and tuck its end under this second wrap to form a second X shape. Tighten by pulling both ends of the rope.

**2. Reef knot**. Used to tie two pieces of cord or rope together. Cross the right end of the rope over and under the left. Then, cross the left end over and under the right. Hold both ends and pull to tighten.

**3. Square lashing**. Used to bind two pieces of wood at right angles. Tie a clove hitch with one end of your rope, then pass the rope over the horizontal pole and under the vertical pole. Weave the rope around the poles three or four times. Take the rope behind the horizontal pole and over the bottom of the vertical pole, then under the horizontal pole and back over the vertical pole. Repeat this process and end by tying another clove hitch.

# ANIMAL ATTACKS!

The Rockies' isolation, climate, and terrain all throw plenty of survival challenges at you. So do some of its creatures. As you travel, look out for any tracks or sounds of large wildlife nearby, as well as smaller critters such as spiders and snakes.

Black and grizzly bears are found in parts of the Rockies. Both are big beasts, with male black bears weighing 550 pounds (250 kg) and grizzlies up to 825 pounds (375 kg). If you come across one, here are your options...

 ## Move away

If you are standing between an adult bear and its cub or cubs, move away quickly as the parent will be at their most dangerous.

 ## Stand tall

If a black bear threatens you, don't look it in the eye. Face it, stand tall, and hold your backpack or a large object above your head to make yourself appear bigger than you are. If it's a grizzly you encounter, do the same, but back away as quickly as you can.

 ## Play dead

If the bear attacks you, fall face down, protect your head and neck, and play dead. The bear may cuff you a few times before it loses interest and lopes away.

# Potential danger

There are many wild creatures in the Rockies, most of which rarely attack, while some will lash out if they are cornered or feel threatened.

**1. Wolves**. Wolves roam parts of the Rockies in packs and mostly hunt at night. If you encounter wolves, don't crouch, turn your back, or flee. Running can trigger a wolf's attack response. As with bears, make yourself appear as big as possible, and shout and growl. If they stand their ground, look to climb a large tree.

**2. Widow spiders**. Several species of black widow spiders are found in the Rockies. The most dangerous common spider in the United States, the female black widow, can inject venom. One bite, although painful, is rarely fatal to humans, but multiple bites can kill.

**3. Wolverine**. Bearlike creatures that are aggressive despite weighing 22 pounds (10 kg), using their claws and jaws to attack.

**4. Bobcat**. Wild cats that are shy and rarely a threat, unless they have cubs. Make noise to scare them off.

**5. Bison**. These cause more injuries in the Rockies than any other large animal. They can weigh as much as a car.

**6. Coyote**. Members of the dog family that are rarely as bold as wolves and are unlikely to attack, even in a pack.

## CREATURE FEATURE: ON TRACK

As you travel, keep an eye on the ground ahead for fresh tracks. These can tell you whether you're following in the paw or hoof prints of animals that might be a danger to you.

**Grizzly bear**  **Gray wolf**  **Bobcat**

# BREAKS AND SPRAINS

The Rockies' tough and varied terrain means you could suffer a trip, fall, or some other injury. Make sure you carry a first aid kit that includes vital supplies such as wrapping and adhesive bandages, and an emergency foil blanket.

With no doctor in sight, you may have to deal with injuries yourself. Here's what you can do with or without a first aid kit...

## Natural antiseptic

If you don't have any antiseptic cream or gel, then look for a small spruce or fir tree. The resin or sticky sap from the tree's bark is mildly antiseptic and can be used on small cuts.

## Mosquito bites

If mosquitoes are proving to be a problem, lavender, garlic, and the common white-flowering yarrow all act as a natural mosquito repellent.

## Burns

Campfires may result in burns. Place the burned area in cool water for 10 minutes or more. Dry the area with care, but leave anything in place that appears stuck to the burned skin. If you have it, place a non-stick dressing pad over the top and wrap fabric bandages over the area.

## Blisters

A friction blister on your feet can make it painful to walk. Clean both the blistered area and a sharp pin with antiseptic liquid. Slide the pin into the edge of the blister and press gently on the other side to squeeze out the fluid. Cover with an adhesive bandage.

## In a sling

If you have severely hurt your hand or arm, you may need to protect it in a sling. Take a triangular piece of cloth, pass it under your injured arm, and put the top corner over your shoulder and around your neck. Take the bottom corner up and knot the two ends together.

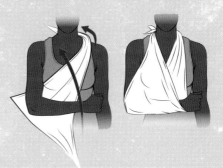

# REAL-LIFE SURVIVOR

In 2017, Madeline Connelly got lost in Montana's Great Bear Wilderness with her dog, Mogi. She hiked up to 10 miles (16 km) a day, gripped branches when crossing slippery ground, spotted grizzly bear tracks, and sheltered at night under trees. She ate lilies and drank creek water. After six days she was spotted and winched to safety by a helicopter.

## CREATURE FEATURE: WESTERN RATTLESNAKE

The only highly venomous native snake in the Rockies, the western rattlesnake is usually found on lower ground where it eats small mammals, reptiles, birds, and birds' eggs. They typically grow to about 3 feet (91 cm) long, but their sandy-brown markings make them hard to spot in the wild. Be careful where you put your hands when clambering up rocky trails, and if you spot a snake, get more than its body length away from it so that it cannot strike.

# ALONE IN THE AMAZON

Welcome to the jungle. The Amazon basin covers a large part of the South American continent and much of it is home to the world's biggest rain forest. Many parts of this vast tropical region are underexplored, barely mapped, and mysterious. What you will find here, if stranded, is dense vegetation and trees, rivers including the mighty Amazon, swamps, and thousands of streams. You'll also see, hear, and encounter an incredible array of wildlife.

**CARIBBEAN SEA**

You are here!

**AMAZON RAIN FOREST**

**PACIFIC OCEAN**

SOUTH AMERICA

**Amazon rain forest fact file**
**Area:** approx. 2,100,000 square miles (5,500,000 km²)—more than ten times the size of Spain!
**Maximum temperature:** 95°F (35°C). Average temperature 82°F (28°C)
**Average rainfall:** 59–138 inches (1,500 – 3,500 mm) per year.

N W E S

For many, a visit to the Amazon is a trip of a lifetime. So how did it turn into a nightmare fight for survival? You may have been a victim of a plane crash or lost your way while trekking with a group. Or you may have been enjoying a river safari before the boat broke down or capsized in rapids or rough water.

## WHAT TO DO FIRST

Hold it together. Although the conditions are tough, many people have survived and been rescued. The main threats you are likely to face are:

- Hot, humid climate
- Dense forest and tough terrain making navigation hard
- Deadly creatures, big and small

- Lack of food
- Quicksand
- Risk of contracting malaria and other tropical diseases

### Where are you?

Think about where you are and whether there might be any settlements nearby. Grab any maps and wrap them in plastic bags so they don't perish in the damp environment.

### See the light

Keep a look out for flashlights, lanterns, lighters, and matches—anything that can light up your way through the forest gloom.

### Grab stuff

If you've ended up here after a crash or boat wreck, scour the wreckage for vital survival items such as insect repellent, water bottles, purifying tablets, rope, netting, a first aid kit, or spare clothes.

### Anyone there?

It's unlikely you traveled into the Amazon totally alone. Could anyone else in your party be nearby? Whistle, shout, and listen hard, above the noise of wildlife, for any faint reply.

## CREATURE FEATURE: ELECTRIC EEL

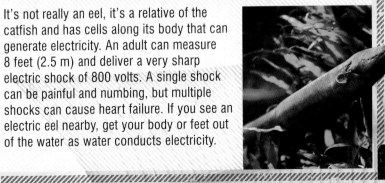

It's not really an eel, it's a relative of the catfish and has cells along its body that can generate electricity. An adult can measure 8 feet (2.5 m) and deliver a very sharp electric shock of 800 volts. A single shock can be painful and numbing, but multiple shocks can cause heart failure. If you see an electric eel nearby, get your body or feet out of the water as water conducts electricity.

# FOREST FRONTIER

Hot, wet, and steamy, the floor of the Amazon rain forest can also be gloomy with little light reaching through the tangled vegetation. Above are layers of bushes and treetops. Back on the ground, wildlife and tough terrain can catch you out if you're not careful.

It's called a rain forest for a reason. Torrential rainfall at times can soak you through, while at other times it's hot and humid. How do you cope with these conditions?

 ## Put gloves on

Gloves in the Amazon? You betcha! Thin but strong sports or adventuring gloves stop your hands from getting bitten, stung, or cut as you move through the jungle.

 ## Wear a hat

A hat, preferably with a broad rim, shields your head and face from dropping insects and spiders. A piece of cloth or a neckerchief can protect you from scratches and bites.

 ## Cover up

Covering up acts as a barrier against bites, stings, and cuts from the sharp-edged leaves and spikes of plants.

 ## Protect your feet

To prevent your feet from getting wet all the time, wrap plastic bags over your socks before putting your shoes or boots on. If you get completely soaked, dry off your clothes, especially your socks, by hanging them up whenever you can, as mold can develop quickly.

# STAYING ALIVE:
## QUICKSAND

On your travels you may come across quicksand (sand mixed usually with water). If you start to sink, don't panic. Many areas of quicksand are less than 3 feet (91 cm) deep.

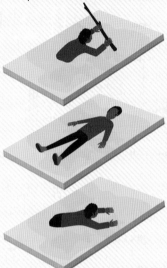

**1. Grab**. Try to grab hold of an overhanging branch or rock and haul yourself out slowly and smoothly. If you jerk and struggle, you are more likely to sink farther.

**2. Float**. If you're stuck in the middle of quicksand, try to increase your body surface area by lying on your back and floating on the top.

**3. Wriggle**. Gradually wriggle your legs free. Then, using slithering or swimming movements of your arms and legs, slowly ease your way to solid ground.

# CREATURE FEATURE:
## ANACONDA

Anacondas coil their enormous muscular bodies around prey and squeeze until it can no longer breathe. These giant snakes can reach more than 20 feet (6 m) long and the heaviest ever found weighed over 200 pounds (90 kg). Stay away from swampland as anacondas are mostly found in and around water. These snakes can go weeks between meals but if one does start winding its way around you, don't breathe out as you may not be able to breathe in again. Use your strength to unwind its coils, working from the tail first.

# CREEPY CRAWLIES

The Amazon is home to millions of insects—an estimated 50,000 different species can exist in a single square mile. Some insects and small creatures can harm you, so protect yourself. Use insect repellent if you have it, and stay alert—your life may depend on it.

Cover as much of your skin as possible. Wear long shirt sleeves, cover your neck, and tuck your pants into your boots or socks to stop small creatures from crawling up your legs. Some of the most common threats are...

 ## Leeches

The Amazon is full of these bloodsuckers which latch onto your skin. Use your fingernail to loosen its grasp before flicking it away. Salt, alcohol, or vinegar can also help make it let go. Clean the wound afterward.

 ## Fire ants

Fire ant stings can feel painful and burning, later turning itchy and blistering. Place a cold, wet cloth on the bitten area for 20 minutes and don't scratch as the blisters may get infected.

 ## Mosquitoes

Mosquito bites can be itchy and irritating, but some mosquitoes can transmit malaria and dengue fever to humans. Keep covered. If out of repellent, smear any exposed body parts in grease, oil, or mud as a temporary barrier. Reapply frequently.

 ## Ticks and botfly

Ticks latch onto your skin. If bitten, use tweezers to grip the tick's head, not the body, and pull it away. Botfly larva can also bore into your body causing pain and swelling. Smear the wound with alcohol or petroleum jelly, or cover using tape. A day or so later, squeeze either side of the wound and pull the larva out by its tail.

# GET PRACTICAL:
# ALL TIED UP

With a veil of netting, mosquito hats may look silly but they can protect you from bites. Use transparent and thin cloth, such as an old or unused mosquito net, to make your own. Drape loosely over the top of your hat and gather and tuck the other end securely inside your shirt.

# CREATURE FEATURE:
# POISON DART FROGS

The many species of poison dart frogs in the Amazon are small (up to 2 inches or 5 cm long), brightly colored, and deadly. Their skin and bodies often contain dangerous poisons. A single golden dart frog has enough poison to kill up to ten adult humans. Don't touch them and wash immediately if you do come into contact.

# CREATURE FEATURE:
# AMAZONIAN GIANT CENTIPEDE

The world's largest centipede can reach a staggering 12 inches (30 cm) long. They are found in leaf litter and soil on the forest floor, as well as in rotting tree trunks and logs. There, they  bide their time waiting to inject prey with their venom, which although not lethal to humans, can cause severe pain and a fever.

# EAT AND SLEEP

Any food you might have on your survival journey will run out soon enough. Fortunately, the Amazon rain forest is a phenomenally fertile place. Its plants can provide you with lots to eat, from edible flowers and roots, to palm hearts and Brazil nuts. The Amazon's trees and plants can also help you build a place to rest.

So where are the best places to bed down for the night and where are you going to find food to eat?

## Bedding down

With so many creatures scuttling around the forest floor, you don't want to be sleeping on the ground. Make a simple platform out of piled branches covered in ferns, large leaves, and palm fronds, and lie on top of this.

## Making camp

Make camp away from stagnant pools of water, which are breeding grounds for mosquitoes and other insects. A smoldering fire, using damp leaves, also helps to keep insects away.

## Multi-purpose Moriche

The moriche palm (also known as the aguaje) is a real larder of a tree. It has vast bundles of fruits (see right), which can be eaten, as can its flower buds. The plant's sap can also be drunk.

## Fruity foods

A vast range of fruits can be found in the Amazon including sacha mango, açaí berries, and passion fruit, which grow on vines. There's also the cupuaçu, which tastes of pineapple and chocolate.

# GET PRACTICAL:
## HOMEMADE HAMMOCK

**1**. Tie one end of a blanket into a knot. Then tie one end of a rope in a tight clove hitch (see p31) just below the blanket knot.

**2**. Wrap the rope around a tree trunk two or three times and then run it above the hammock across to another tree. Wrap it around the second trunk before repeating step one with the other blanket end.

# CREATURE FEATURE:
## JAGUARS

While you're sleeping, the biggest cats in South America may be hunting. Jaguars can swim, climb, and leap with great agility—and kill with a single bite of their powerful jaws. Fortunately, they tend to only attack humans if cornered or threatened. Keep an eye out for their distinctive gold and black markings, and stay well away.

# REAL-LIFE SURVIVOR

Twenty-two-year-old Yossi Ghinsburg was left alone in the Amazon after his raft capsized in rapids. He survived for three weeks before a search party rescued him. He ate berries and fruits that had fallen to the forest floor and scavenged eggs laid by wild chickens on the ground. He was bitten by insects, nearly drowned in a swamp, and once came face to face with a jaguar. Using a lighter, he set fire to an insect repellent spray to scare the big cat away.

# RAIN FOREST WATERWAYS

The mighty Amazon River flows some 4,000 miles (6,500 km) through South America and is more than 6 miles (10 km) wide in some places. Yet, it is just one of many rivers and streams in the rain forest. More than 1,100 rivers and streams flow into the Amazon in total.

You may need to cross a river rather than travel along it. Perhaps the terrain looks better on the other side or you can see smoke or hear people making noises. Take time to scout the river before you cross and consider the following...

## Point of entry

Avoid crossing where there are slippery rocks, heavy mud, or the water is flowing fast. Sand bars in the middle of the river give you a target to head to and split the river up into smaller, more easily crossable channels.

## Valuables

Put any items that you need to keep dry, such as maps and electronics, in a plastic bag. Make sure there are no holes and roll up the top of the bag tightly. Secure it with a rubber band or bungee cord, or tie it up with a vine.

## Exit point

Look for an easy exit point out of the river on the other bank. Aim to enter the river 45 degrees upstream of that point to allow for the water carrying you downstream.

## Boots on

Keep your boots on for grip and support—you can dry them later. Lean into the current as you cross and use a stout branch for support upstream of your feet.

# GET PRACTICAL:
## TRAVEL DOWNSTREAM

If a river flows gently, consider making a simple wooden raft by lashing some logs together (see p65). Or, if you have a machete or axe, make a dugout canoe. Fashion a wooden paddle by lashing two short logs to the end of a tree branch. Once on the water be aware of dangers and if the river starts speeding up, paddle quickly to shore.

## Make a float

You can use a pair of pants as a flotation aid. (1) Tie the pant legs tightly and enter the water with the pants held over your back.

**1.** **2.** **3.**

(2) Swing the pants up and over your head, and while they're full of air slam them into the water. (3) Finally, squeeze and knot the pants' waistline to keep the air in before lying over the top of them.

# CREATURE FEATURE:
## RED-BELLIED PIRANHA

Schools of these 8–14-inch- (20–35-cm)-long meat-eaters will hunt creatures larger than themselves, using their sharp, triangular teeth to bite and tear. Piranhas rarely attack humans, but do so mostly in the dry season (May to October) when food is short. If you have to cross a river that contains piranhas, throw a dead fish or mammal into the water downstream from where you intend to cross.

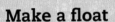

# SEEKING SAFETY

You may know where you are going, but if you are unsure, the key tip is to follow a river downstream to increase your chances of finding a settlement by the river or people in boats who can help you. If you're in dense jungle, try to locate a stream and follow it downhill. It should flow into a bigger waterway.

So how do you improve your chances of finding other people who can lead you to safety?

## Listen carefully

Listen for any signs of human activity. A chugging motor sound may signal that a river and motorboats are nearby. Whirring chainsaws and crashing timbers can lead you to forestry or logging workers. As you approach, call out and be wary of falling trees.

## Rain forest peoples

Help may be near, even in the densest jungle. More than 400 different native peoples live in the Amazon rain forest. Many are forest experts and some partly or entirely live off the land. If you encounter a rain forest dweller, try not to startle them. Hold your hands out to the side to show you mean no harm, but need help.

## Leave markings

Mark your route by leaving small pieces of brightly colored clothing, if you have plenty to spare. Snap off tree branches or carve marks onto trees at eye level for others to see.

## Look out

Keep an eye out for fresh footprints on the forest floor or on a river bank.

# CREATURE FEATURE:
## BLACK CAIMAN

That large knobbly log in the water may actually be the Amazon's largest predator. Growing up to 16½ feet (5 m) long and weighing up to 880 pounds (400 kg), caimans use their powerful jaws to grab and rip their prey, which they then try to swallow whole. Black caimans hunt only at night, but attacks on people result in several deaths and a number of injuries each year.

# REAL-LIFE SURVIVOR

On Christmas Eve 1971, an airliner carrying 17-year-old Juliane Koepcke and 91 other passengers was struck by lightning and fell apart. Still belted to her seat, Juliane plunged around 10,500 feet (3,200 m) through the air and crashed into the Amazon rain forest. As the only survivor, she would spend 11 days alone in the Amazon with her collar bone broken and right eye swollen shut.

Remembering that heading downhill in the jungle leads to water and water leads to civilization, Juliane followed a stream which became a river, staying wary of snakes and caimans lurking by the water's edge. She was wearing a short summer dress so she suffered many insect bites, some of which became infected. On discovering a boat and a hut by the river, she poured gasoline into her wounds and removed more than 30 botfly larva from her arm. She was later discovered at the hut by logging workers and airlifted to safety.

"SUDDENLY THE NOISE STOPPED AND I WAS OUTSIDE THE PLANE. I WAS IN A FREEFALL, STRAPPED TO MY SEAT. I COULD SEE THE CANOPY OF THE JUNGLE SPINNING TOWARD ME."

# STRANDED IN A POLAR WILDERNESS

The region around the South Pole is mostly made up of the icy desert continent of Antarctica as well as the bitterly cold Southern Ocean and islands. The northern polar region, within the Arctic Circle, is a mixture of chilly Arctic Ocean, ice sheets, and the northernmost lands of Europe, Canada, Russia, and Alaska.

Arctic
Circle

ARCTIC
OCEAN

North
Pole

ANTARCTICA

South
Pole

SOUTHERN OCEAN

### Arctic Circle fact file
**Area:** 5,600,000 square miles (14,500,000 km$^2$)
**Minimum temperature:** -58°F (-50°C)
**Average rainfall:** 10 inches (25 cm) per year

### Antarctica fact file
**Area:** 5,400,000 square miles (14,000,000 km$^2$)
**Minimum temperature:** -128.6°F (-89.2°C)
**Average rainfall:** 6½ inches (16.5 cm) per year

How might you end up stranded in a polar region? You might be part of an expedition that has gone desperately wrong, or your ship may have sunk. Planes, caught in storms, have crashed in the Arctic. Other people have gotten lost visiting a settlement or base, when a sudden blizzard separated them from others.

## WHAT TO DO FIRST

With cold threatening to gnaw away at you right from the start, acting quickly is vital for survival. The main dangers you face are:

- Intense cold potentially leading to hypothermia
- Frostbite
- Snow blindness
- Blizzards
- Avalanches
- Lack of food

### Get warm

Seek ways to keep warm. Put extra clothes on, find a shelter, and make sure your hands, feet, and face are well covered to avoid frostbite (see pp50-51).

### What can you work with?

Salvage any useful materials before snowfall covers them—from string, a shovel, and extra socks to flashlights, a stove, and fuel.

### Think ahead

Are you likely to be saved where you are? A crashed plane a short distance from a town is likely to attract rescuers. Staying with a stricken boat or land vehicle can guarantee you shelter.

### Get some food

Gather as much food as you can. Choose foods which are high in energy. This is no time for a diet! You'll need the calories because of the extra energy needed in these harsh conditions.

## CREATURE FEATURE:
# KILLER WHALE

One of the few creatures found in both polar regions is the orca, or killer whale. At up to 26 feet (8 m) long, they can take down the biggest seals, and even great white sharks, with chilling ease. Orcas rarely attack humans but they may capsize boats, throwing you into the freezing waters.

# FIGHTING THE FREEZE

Temperatures vary wildly in the polar regions. Summers in the southern parts of the Arctic Circle can be a mild and balmy 59–68ºF (15–20ºC), but in winter, average temperatures dip and stay below 0ºC for months at a time. The weather is even harsher in Antarctica, with temperatures of -22ºF or -40ºF (-30ºC or -40ºC) common in winter—that's twice as cold as your kitchen freezer!

So, fighting the freeze may be your fiercest polar challenge of all. Think about the warm clothing you have—wearing it in the right way can make a crucial difference...

### Layer up

Wear lots of layers of clothing, as air trapped between the layers helps to insulate you from the cold. Tracksuit bottoms under windproof pants and several pairs of socks all help to keep you warm. Tuck your top layers into your bottom layers and your pant legs into your socks to stop heat from escaping.

### Cover your face

Keep as much of your face out of the cold as possible. Wear a woolly hat, scarf, and draw your coat hood up tight. Use lip balm or vaseline to protect your lips and wear high protection sunblock on your face.

### Protect your hands

Your hands are vulnerable in the extreme cold. If you can, wear a thin inner pair and a thicker outer pair of gloves. In extreme cold, mittens can be worn over the two pairs of gloves. Thick, woolly socks can act as temporary mittens.

### Don't touch

In extreme cold, avoid touching metal surfaces, such as a tent pole, with your bare hands. Your skin can freeze onto the metal instantly.

# GET PRACTICAL:
## MAKE A BALACLAVA

To prevent frostbite to your ears, nose, and cheeks, make a simple balaclava. Cut eye and mouth holes out of a pant leg or the arm of a woolly sweater. Bunch one end up with a rubber band or string.

### Frostbite

Frostbite occurs when blood stops flowing to a part of your body. Frostnip is the first sign, with areas stinging or feeling prickly before turning pale and numb. Frostbite goes deeper and often affects fingers, toes, the nose, and ears. In severe cases, it can leave body parts dead. If you feel frostnip, you need to get warm and dry quickly, before frostbite develops.

# CREATURE FEATURE:
## MUSK OX

The thick coats of these large Arctic plant-eaters demonstrate layering in nature. The outer layer of their coats is made up of thick, long hairs, with a packed layer of denser, shorter hairs underneath. The inner layer is used by Arctic peoples to spin qiviut wool, which is up to eight times warmer than sheep's wool. Keep your distance, as an adult musk ox can weigh up to 880 pounds (400 kg) and may charge at you if threatened.

READ ABOUT HOW TO TREK ACROSS SNOW AND ICE ON P56.

# WILD WINDS

The numbing cold is only part of your polar challenge. Wild winds and snowstorms can restrict your every move unless you are prepared. Strong winds can increase your rate of heat loss, making you feel far colder. This is called wind chill and it can be deadly —a 25 mph (40 km/h) wind when the temperature is 5°F (-15°C), for instance, can make the conditions feel like -31°F (-35°C).

 Snowfall and sweat can build up and make you wet. Your body loses heat more quickly to water than air. Here's how to avoid getting wet...

 ## Reduce sweat

Adjust your clothing layers to stop sweat. Open a zipper or remove and carry one inner clothing layer.

 ## Freeze-dry

Some military survival experts suggest letting wet clothes freeze. Once stiff, it can be easier to remove the ice by shaking the clothing hard and beating it.

 ## Dry your boots

If you have a fire, lift out warm (not baking hot) stones using two sticks and slide them into your wet boots to dry them out.

 ## Avoid trenchfoot

If your unclean feet stay wet for long periods, it can result in this painful foot infection. Keep your feet dry when you can, change your socks, and dry wet ones over a fire or by tying them to your body when trekking.

## Blizzards

These severe windy snowstorms are serious life threateners. During a blizzard, make sure your back is turned into the wind, your head bowed, and face covered to stop debris from flying into your eyes. Seek shelter and keep a shovel or stick handy to dig yourself out if the blizzard buries you in snow.

## GET PRACTICAL:
# AVOID THE GLARE

Snow blindness is caused by glare from the sun reflecting off bright white snow and ice. Your eyes can feel sore, teary, and painful and your eyesight may be affected. Wear ski goggles or wraparound sunglasses. Got no goggles? Improvise. Cut small, narrow slits into flexible tree bark, such as birch, or in duct tape strips. Add holes at either end and tie around your head with string or a spare boot lace.

# REAL-LIFE SURVIVOR

While trekking across Antarctica in the 1920s, the Danish explorer Peter Freuchen was buried under a giant mound of snow caused by a powerful blizzard. Without any tools to help him, Peter improvised. He used his poop—which was frozen solid—as a chisel, and chipped his way out of the frozen snow.

# SHELTER AND WATER

A shelter can protect you from blizzards and keep you warmer than out in the open. It's also vital to keep hydrated to help your body cope with the extreme conditions, and to help your heart pump warm blood around your body.

A large cave or abandoned hut is great, but what if you only have snow, ice, and the occasional tree to work with? Fortunately, there are many different types of shelter you can make.

### Igloo

Used by Arctic Inuits, these secure and surprisingly warm shelters are made from blocks of packed snow used as large bricks to form a circular dome. They take many hours to construct.

### Quinzee

Simpler than an igloo, you mound and pack snow up around all your possessions to form a 5–6½-foot- (1.5–2-m-) tall half-ball shape on the ground. Push sticks 16–20 inches (40–50 cm) into your structure to act as a depth guide. Then burrow down below and hollow your shelter out from the inside.

### Snow cave

Need to act quickly? Burrow into a firm snow bank and create a thick, curving roof for strength. Poke several holes through the roof for air. Use your backpack or blocks of packed snow as a door and keep your shovel or other digging tool, such as a cooking pot, inside with you.

# GET PRACTICAL:
# KEEP HYDRATED

You may find it hard to guzzle down water in the extreme cold, but it's important you do so.

**Snow Go**
Eating fresh snow or ice should be a last resort as it will further cool your body and lower its temperature. In the summer, lakes and streams provide plenty of water. In the winter, seek out meltwaters —water melting from the edges of ice formations. Snow and ice can be heated by a fire or stove to create fresh drinking water. If you don't have a fire, you can pack snow in a bag and hang it above ground to let it melt gradually in the sun.

# CREATURE FEATURE:
# POLAR BEAR

More than 25,000 polar bears live wild in the Arctic. Weighing up to 1,320 pounds (600 kg), they are supreme hunters, able to sniff out the scent of prey more than ½ mile (1 km) away. Ravenous polar bears occasionally attack humans, so keep plenty of distance. If a bear approaches, use a signal flare or wave a flaming torch, and shout and stamp, to deter from getting closer.

LEARN MORE ABOUT MAKING FIRES AND KEEPING THEM GOING (SEE P28).

# MAKING A MOVE

Polar landscapes can sometimes seem featureless, making it hard for you to keep to a route by eye alone. Try to pick distant landmarks ahead, such as a mountain peak, and if you have a compass, use it to stay on track.

Trekking across snow and ice can be hard work and exhausting. What can you do to keep moving?

### Keep it steady

Don't wear yourself out too early. Try to move at an even pace that you can keep up for a long time.

### Use poles

Walking poles or cut tree branches help you balance and test the terrain ahead for thin ice and snow bridges.

### Make snowshoes

Boots can plunge deep into soft snow. Spread the load of your body weight over a bigger area by making simple snowshoes from flexible tree saplings bent around and with their ends lashed together. Then use lots of cord and smaller pieces of wood tied across the frame to brace it and tie your boot to the snowshoe.

### Look at the ice

Pay attention to the color of the ice ahead of you. White = thick, mature ice which is safe to cross. Gray = thinner ice (often 4–6 inches or 10–15 cm thick) which may only just support your weight. Black = usually newly formed, thin, and not able to bear your weight.

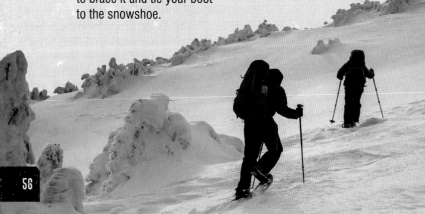

## STAYING ALIVE:
# FIND A FRIEND

Don't give up hope. Plenty of people have been rescued by air, sea, or land after days in polar wildernesses.

**1. Snow SOS.** Spell SOS in the snow by marking it with bright colors, such as blood from a dead animal.

**2. Timber!** If in the southern Arctic forests, stay alert for sights or sounds of logging activity which may lead you to forest workers.

**3. Sled search.** In the Arctic, look out for sled tracks. Arctic peoples and adventurers use dog-drawn sleds to cross icy wildernesses.

**4. Ace base.** Antarctica has over 70 science research stations and visiting tourists in summer. Look out for tracks made by vehicles traveling to and from these bases.

## CREATURE FEATURE:
# LEOPARD SEALS

Insulated from the cold by a thick layer of fatty blubber, leopard seals can grow up to 11½ feet (3.5 m) long. Although almost half of their diet is shrimp, like krill, they also have a taste for bigger prey, including penguins and other seals. Attacks on humans do occur, so steer clear of the ice's edge where they could pounce and pull you into the water.

# TREACHEROUS TERRAIN

Not enough challenges already for you? Don't worry, polar lands and waters possess yet more hurdles and pitfalls to threaten your chances of survival!

 In mountainous areas, masses of snow can slide and tumble down a slope, picking up ferocious speed and power. These avalanches can be fatal unless you take quick action...

## Move away
Move sideways and away from the center of the avalanche where the snow moves fastest.

## Swim out
If caught up in the snow, try swimming movements with your arms and legs to stay on or near the top of the snow.

## Take cover
Lie flat and cover your mouth and nose with your arms. When the avalanche stops, immediately clear space around your head so you can breathe.

## Grab a tree
Try to grab onto a stout tree, branch, or rock, or shelter underneath a rocky overhang.

# GET PRACTICAL:
## CROSSING A CREVASSE

A crevasse is a deep crack in a glacier or ice sheet. A snow bridge is drifting snow that has covered and hidden a crevasse. Both can be lethal. To be safe, prod the terrain ahead with a long pole.

**1.** Turn your long walking pole sideways if you feel yourself falling through a gap in the ice. If the pole catches on either side of the hole, use it to haul yourself out.

**2.** Chilly water below ice can be a killer, so if you fall in, get out as quick as you can. Kick violently and place your upper body and arms on the ice. Haul yourself out and roll in dry snow to dry off.

# REAL-LIFE SURVIVOR

Ernest Shackleton was a polar veteran, but he could not have foreseen the terrible trials his third expedition in 1914–16 would go through. It started when his ship, *Endurance*, became trapped in ice for ten months, some distance off the Antarctic coast. The ship eventually sank, leaving all 28 men stranded in raging blizzards.

Hauling three heavy wooden lifeboats, the crew lived off the ship's rations, as well as seals and penguins they hunted. Four months after their ship sank, the expedition sailed to uninhabited Elephant Island. There, Shackleton took five men, in one lifeboat, on a terrifying 17-day, 795-mile- (1,280-km-) long voyage through stormy seas to South Georgia island, where help was found. All 28 men survived their ordeal.

# MAROONED IN THE PACIFIC OCEAN

The Pacific Ocean is the world's biggest ocean—and you're stuck right in the middle of it. This vast expanse of water covers more than 30 percent of the entire planet's surface. It is an average 13,000 feet (4,000 m) deep and is home to almost 30,000 islands. These islands range from large landmasses to thousands of smaller rocky outcrops and volcanic peaks. Getting to know your island will be crucial to your chances of survival.

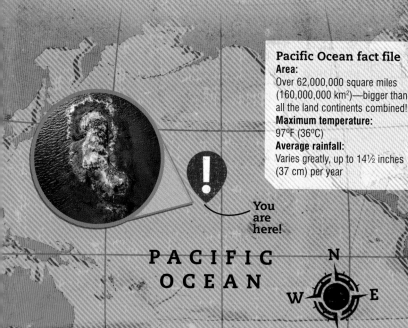

**Pacific Ocean fact file**
**Area:**
Over 62,000,000 square miles (160,000,000 km$^2$)—bigger than all the land continents combined!
**Maximum temperature:**
97°F (36°C)
**Average rainfall:**
Varies greatly, up to 14½ inches (37 cm) per year

You are here!

PACIFIC OCEAN

N
W E
S

How did you get here? The most likely causes are boating disasters, such as your vessel sinking after striking rocks or getting caught in a storm. A handful of desert island survivors are dumped on an island after a mutiny on their ship, or have survived their plane crashing into the ocean.

## WHAT TO DO FIRST

Sun, sea, and, possibly, palm-fringed beaches—it may sound like you're on a tropical dream holiday, but this is no time to kick back and relax. Dangers you face include:

- Lack of food
- Lack of cover from the sweltering sun
- Mosquitoes and other disease-carrying insects
- Lack of water
- Dangerous sea and land creatures

### Move on up

Don't rest on the shore as you could get cut off from land by the high tide. Move yourself above the high tide line where seaweed and other sea life have been deposited by waves.

### Seek shelter

Finding shelter is a priority. Look for a forested grove or cave, but not one that can be reached by the high tide.

### Find water

Unless you've arrived with floating barrels full of water, you'll need to find a good water source that isn't contaminated with sea water.

### Look for signs of life

Is your island actually deserted? Scout out any signs of human activity, such as smoke in the distance, freshly discarded trash or tracks made by a vehicle.

## CREATURE FEATURE: BLUE-RINGED OCTOPUS

Small and pretty, but deadly, these 5–8 inch (12–20 cm) long creatures are found lurking in rocky crevices, tidal pools, and coral reefs. Chemicals in their venom are thought to be more than 1,000 times more toxic than cyanide. Its bite can lead to loss of eyesight, breathing problems, paralysis, and even death.

# SHORE SURVIVAL

Your island's shoreline can be incredibly useful—it's where you can leave distress signals or find food in rock pools, such as crabs, shrimp or edible seaweed. However, there are also dangers on the shore, including razor-sharp coral or stones and strong, narrow currents, known as rip tides, that can drag you out to sea.

Ocean waves can wash up a wide range of useful materials. Comb the shore regularly and you might find the following...

### Driftwood

Invaluable if your island lacks big trees, large pieces of wood can be useful for shelter, tools, or fires. Seek out nails or staples, which can make needles and fishing hooks.

### Food flotsam

Many seaweed species are edible and reach the shore in tangled masses. Coconuts with their waterproof husk are naturally buoyant and can float long distances.

### Wreckage

If your boat or plane was wrecked close to the island, some useful items might reach the shore. Look out for sharp pieces of metal you could use as a knife, or containers for storing water.

### Plastic containers

Bottles, boxes, and floating buoys that have come loose from their boats can all be used to store water.

# CREATURE FEATURE:
## ROCK POOL RESIDENTS

As you explore the fringes of your island, be careful where you step and sit. Many creatures in the shallows and rock pools can inflict painful injuries.

**1. Sea anemones**. Many species can give you a painful sting. Parts of their tentacles can also break off in your body and cause infections.

**2. Fire coral**. These can serve up a toxic sting from their thread-like tubes. Some species are razor-sharp to touch and can slice your legs, hands, and feet.

**3. Cone shells**. Pretty but deadly, these can deliver a sting full of venom that can numb your body and even cause paralysis, heart failure, and death.

**4. Stonefish**. With its crusty covering, the stonefish cannot easily be seen. Dangerous venom from the sharp spines along its back makes this fish among the most lethal of all.

# REAL-LIFE SURVIVOR

In September 1704, 28-year-old sailor Alexander Selkirk fell out with the captain of his ship in the South Pacific. He was left marooned and alone on one of the Juan Fernández Islands, over 400 miles (650 km) from the coast of South America.

After weeks on the shore, living off fish and "spiny lobsters" (a type of crayfish), Selkirk finally moved inland. There, he built two huts and ate wild plums and root vegetables. He also hunted wild goats and fished. He used the goats' hides to fashion new clothes until he was finally rescued in 1709. Selkirk would become the real-life inspiration for the story of fictional desert islander Robinson Crusoe.

# EXPLORING YOUR NEW HOME

While your best hope of rescue lies on the shore, you may need to head inland to stay alive. Exploring your island can lead to vital discoveries such as an abandoned hut or ship, or a grove of fruit trees. The most important, life-saving discovery of all may be a plentiful source of water.

If you find water, is it safe to drink? If you can build a fire, it's best to boil water before drinking it. This will also allow you to cook tough vegetation into more digestible meals. Here's what you can do to find fresh water...

## Search for a fresh stream

Look for a stream emptying into the sea and trace it back to where it is fast-flowing to collect water.

## Make a rain trap

You can make a simple rain trap by folding a wide, glossy leaf a little down the middle, to funnel water down into a container.

## Collect rainwater

Leave out containers to collect rainwater. Stretch out plastic bags, waterproof garments, and tarpaulins, and weigh down with stones in the middle to funnel rain into the center (see p89).

## Dig down

Above the high tide line on the island, you could dig down for water. You may have to dig for several feet to find water, which should be boiled before drinking.

## Farther afield

If you see another island, only consider heading to it if your current home lacks water, food, shelter, or people. Island hopping can be a big risk, so ask yourself: do the islands have rocky or sandy coastlines? Have you seen sharks in the waters? Are tides and currents strong?

## GET PRACTICAL:
## RAFT CLASS

Build a simple raft using two 5–8-foot- (1.5–2.5-m-) long logs or bamboo canes lashed together with smaller branches. Use thick vines for lashing if you lack rope. Make your raft wider than it is long and lash bundles of bamboo to either side of the main raft platform. These will help make your raft more stable in the water.

## CREATURE FEATURE:
## REEF SHARKS

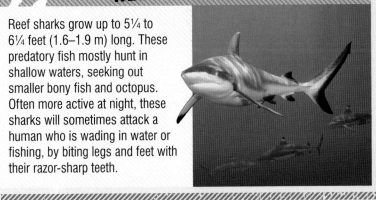

Reef sharks grow up to 5¼ to 6¼ feet (1.6–1.9 m) long. These predatory fish mostly hunt in shallow waters, seeking out smaller bony fish and octopus. Often more active at night, these sharks will sometimes attack a human who is wading in water or fishing, by biting legs and feet with their razor-sharp teeth.

# LIVING OFF THE LAND

You may hope for rescue within days, but if your island is a long way from shipping lanes and flight paths, you may have to prepare yourself for a long stay. If that's the case, you'll need to build a shelter and secure plenty of food supplies.

 If you have or discover food, remember it can spoil quickly in the hot sun. So that it lasts much longer, you can preserve all sorts of foods in the following ways...

 ## Drying

The meat of a coconut as well as other plants and fish can be dried in the hot sun. Make a simple frame of wood to keep them off the ground as they dry.

 ## Smoking

Build a simple spit over a smoky fire by resting a long pole on two forked branches. To make a smoky fire, use slightly green hardwood, let the fire smolder, and don't make it too big or roaring hot. Slices of meat, fish, and fruits can be placed on the pole, smoked, and preserved.

 ## Adding salt or citrus

You can obtain salt by putting some seawater in a shallow container and letting the water evaporate. The salt can be rubbed into fish to help preserve it. If you have lime or lemon trees on your island, soak vegetables in their juice to preserve them.

# STAYING ALIVE:
## TREE-MENDOUS FOODS

Many tropical Pacific islands are packed with fast-growing trees and other valuable plants. Mangos, bananas, and guava are all possible food sources, as are the following four foods.

**1. Bamboo.** The young shoots of this plant can be eaten raw or cooked. Peel away the outer husk like you would do with an ear of corn to get at the tender shoot inside.

**2. Plantain.** This relative of the banana can also be eaten raw,

but tastes better when cooked whole in the embers of a fire.

**3. Breadfruit.** These green fruits can reach up to 12 inches (30 cm) in diameter. The seeds inside need to be roasted, but the fleshy pulp can be eaten raw.

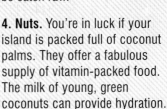

**4. Nuts.** You're in luck if your island is packed full of coconut palms. They offer a fabulous supply of vitamin-packed food. The milk of young, green coconuts can provide hydration.

# GET PRACTICAL:
## BUILD A BASE

If there's no suitable cave or natural shelter, you'll have to build one. Site it close to food and water supplies to save your energy.

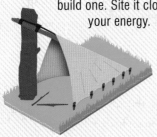

**A-frame lean-to:** Place a large fallen branch up against a tree trunk to form the roof ridge. Lean smaller branches along its length and then cover with lots of dense foliage.

MAKE A SIMPLE FOUR-FORKED SPEAR FROM BAMBOO CANE (SEE P91).

# SHIP AHOY!

Stories are told of desert island survivors sending messages in bottles which lead to their rescue...but they're mostly just that—tall tales and fiction. It could take months or even years for the ocean tides to deposit a bottle into the hands of someone. And bottles are just too useful for you to cast off into the water.

So if you're marooned on an island what are the quickest and most effective ways to attract attention? Try the following...

## Send a signal

If you see a ship or plane, use a mirror, piece of metal, or any shiny surface to reflect the sun's rays in the direction of the vessel.

## Spell it out

Make SOS or HELP messages out of leaves and seaweed on exposed shorelines, weighted down by stones. Place your message above the high tide line so that it will last.

## Think ahead

Unless you are on a flight path for planes between other islands, your most likely source of rescue will come from the sea. Make sure you are prepared in advance, in case a ship appears on the horizon.

## Move to another location

Place messages on different sides of the island as you won't know which direction help may come from. Remember to wave your arms if a ship or plane comes into view.

## Signal fires

If you have matches or a way of lighting fires easily, you should build signal fires on key points of your island.

**2**. Put tinder on the platform and cover the tripod to protect it from rain, or store dry tinder separately so it can be lit if you spot a plane or ship.

**1**. Lash three branches to form a tripod. Then build a platform with smaller sticks.

**3**. Once each fire is going, heap on green palms and other leaves. These generate lots of thick dark smoke which might be spotted by distant planes and ships.

# REAL-LIFE SURVIVORS

After waves capsized their yacht in April 2016, three men swam about 2 miles (3.2 km) to Fanadik, an island in Micronesia. After three days, their large "help" sign made out of palm leaves on the island's shore was spotted by a Navy plane, which led to their rescue.

## CREATURE FEATURE:
## COCONUT CRAB

Also known as the robber crab, these armored monsters can weigh about 9 pounds (4 kg). That's plenty of crab meat, but their giant pincers can clamp onto a limb and stay there painfully for a long time. The crab has a keen sense of smell and is particularly attracted to coconuts and bananas, so if you see one scuttling away or clambering up a tree, you can follow at a distance to find food yourself.

SEND GPS COORDINATES BEFORE YOUR SMARTPHONE GIVES UP (SEE P23).

69

# DESERTED IN THE AUSTRALIAN OUTBACK

The Australian outback is both beautiful and forbidding. The vast interior of Australia varies, from hot sandy deserts to semi-tropical savannah and the forests of the Great Western Woodlands—an area bigger than England. Whatever the landscape, the outback is mostly deserted, with roads and towns very few and far between.

PACIFIC OCEAN

OUTBACK

You are here!

**A U S T R A L I A**

INDIAN OCEAN

N
W · E
S

## Outback fact file
**Area:** Approximately 2,500,000 square miles (6,500,000 km²)—that's 18 times the size of Germany!
**Maximum temperature:** 113°F (45°C)
**Average rainfall:** 6–16 inches (15–40 cm) per year

How did you end up alone in Australia's harsh interior? Perhaps you had an accident in a car or ran out of fuel? Maybe your plane crash-landed in the middle of nowhere. Or perhaps you veered off track and couldn't find your way back. Whatever happened, it is going to take nerve and endurance to get out.

# WHAT TO DO FIRST

Don't panic. Try to think straight. Salvaging everything you can from your vehicle (see p72) may provide you with valuable tools and supplies. The main threats you face are:

- Hot sun
- Lack of water and food
- Extreme isolation—you can be hundreds of miles from the nearest settlement
- Bushfires
- Hazardous creatures

## Think back

Recall any road signs, settlements, or water sources you have seen. You may need to head in their direction.

## Power up

Any power left in your vehicle or smartphone? If so, try to get a GPS fix on your location (see p23) and send messages for help if possible.

## Find shade

Seek shade to avoid sunburn and, if water is scarce, to minimize your sweating.

## Hit the highway

If you find yourself near a major road, stay near it and keep your eyes and ears open and alert for vehicles. In the short term, it is your best bet of an early rescue.

## CREATURE FEATURE:
# RED KANGAROO

One of Australia's national symbols, red kangaroos dwarf other roo species. At up to 9 feet (2.8 m) long, an adult male can reach speeds of over 25 mph (40 km/h). They may look lovable, but they have powerful hind legs with claws that can rip you open. They can also bite and jab with their front paws. If you see an aggressive red roo, crouch to show you are not a threat and retreat quickly.

# SALVAGE OPERATION

It is likely you are stranded in the Australian bush because your motor vehicle crashed or broke down and can't be repaired. Don't just abandon it without a thought. If your vehicle is safe to approach (i.e. no fuel leaks or risk of fire), scour it from top to bottom, looking for vital items including water containers, food, flashlights with batteries, a first aid kit, and tools.

In an abandoned car, seat belts or electrical wiring can be used as rope. What else can you salvage?

## Windows

The top edges of car windows are often unpolished and can be used to sharpen knife blades.

## Hubcaps

Metal hubcaps can make good cooking dishes and rainwater collectors. A pair of pliers can grip their rim to make a saucepan handle.

## Reflectors and mirrors

Pry open a headlight. The silver reflector inside should come away and will work well as a mirror to signal to rescuers (see p21). Alternatively, remove the rearview mirror to use.

## Seats

Seat covers can be cut away and used to make a simple poncho or groundsheet to stay dry and slightly warmer at night. Seat padding can be used to insulate you from the ground when resting.

## Stay or go

If you have to leave your vehicle, put the hood up and write "HELP" or "SOS" on it and the car's sides with oil, paint, or whatever pigment you can find. Add the date and an arrow in the direction you intend to head. Any potential rescuer can then estimate how far away you might be.

## CREATURE FEATURE: SALTWATER CROCODILE

"Salties" are powerful hunters that grow up to 20 feet (6 m) in length. Their large jaws contain over 60 teeth and can clamp down with fearsome pressure on prey, crushing bones and bodies. Attacks on humans can be sudden and often occur after the dry season (September to January) when food is hardest to come by. Contrary to popular belief, you can outrun a saltie, providing you react sharply and sprint in a straight line. If you are caught or cornered, your best bet is to strike or gouge their eyes, as the rest of their head is heavily protected.

## REAL-LIFE SURVIVOR

In 2007, 53-year-old David George fell and was knocked unconscious in the outback. When he came to, he found himself surrounded by saltwater crocodiles. He quickly climbed a tree and stayed there for six days with the crocs lurking beneath. He only had the sandwiches in his pack to eat and obtained water from leaves. David built a platform out of branches to lie on and, on hearing helicopters, reflected sunlight using a metal tin and covered branches with toilet paper to attract attention.

# BUSH TUCKER

For thousands of years, Aboriginal peoples wandered through the outback, surviving by living off the land. They caught and ate marsupials, such as wallabies and kangaroos, but also learned to recognize which plants could provide valuable food and medicine. This is sometimes referred to today as bush tucker.

 You need to be vigilant, however, as some outback plants are poisonous. What should you avoid and how do you check if something is safe to eat?

 ### Test on your skin
If you think something might be safe to eat, place a small bit first on the inside of your elbow. Wait 15 minutes to see if a rash develops.

 ### Stay away from fungi
Avoid eating mushrooms and other fungi or anything that smells or tastes of almonds.

 ### Put it on your tongue
Bush tucker experts will hold a piece of plant on their tongue. If there's no burning or stinging sensation, they may chew, but not swallow.

 ### Wait a few hours
If there's still no burning or stinging, they may swallow the bit of plant and wait a few hours. If they don't feel sick or have diarrhea, they may eat another small portion.

# Grub's up

It may not look appealing, but the witchetty grub, which can grow up to 15 cm long, is packed with protein and can help stave off hunger. You'll have to dig down as they're found in and around the roots of the witchetty bush. They can be eaten raw but are more palatable roasted on a fire, with a crispy skin and chewy white meat inside.

## STAYING ALIVE: FRUIT AND NUTS

Look out for energy-rich fruits and berries, as well as nuts, which are high in calories and protein.

**1. Lilly-pilly** (left). The fruits of this evergreen tree are bland but can be eaten raw and contain a lot of fiber and nutrients.

**2. Macadamia nuts.** These nuts are high in calories and nutrients, but their shells are tough to crack. Place the nut, seam up, in a hole or depression in a rock and strike with a stone.

## CREATURE FEATURE: HONEY ANTS

Honey ants are so-named because they store flower nectar in balloon-like pouches, which eventually dwarf the ant itself. They regurgitate this sweet liquid to feed other ants in their nest, but you can get a small sugar rush by eating these pouches. Remember, surviving is no time to be squeamish!

# FIRE!

A fire can be key to your survival. Choose a clear area, dig a hole in the ground, and surround it with a ring of rocks to keep it contained. Collect and prepare fuel by snapping branches into smaller, usable lengths. Look for dry, thin materials which will catch alight easily. Dry mosses, grasses, tree bark, paper, and clothing fluff all make good tinder.

If you don't have matches or a lighter to start your fire, what other items can you use to get flames going?

### Glasses

Spectacle lenses or a magnifying glass held close to a bundle of tinder can focus the Sun's rays and cause the tinder to catch fire.

### Wires and a battery

Attach electrical wires to the terminals of a 9-volt battery. Holding the insulated part of the wires, touch the two bare ends together next to the tinder so that small sparks can set it alight.

### Plastic bottle

In strong sun, a water-filled clear plastic bottle can act like a lens. Place a folded piece of paper close to your tinder. Use the bottle to focus sunlight on the darkest part of the paper—if you have white paper, darken it with a pen or dry earth. Once the paper starts smoldering, add more paper. Repeat and gently fan the air to encourage the flames before using a stick to push the paper into your fire.

## Look after your fire

Gently blow or fan your tinder, add more tinder, and once flames appear, add your smallest, driest twigs. Gradually build up your fire and keep it going by feeding it with fuel. After use, always fully extinguish any fire. Cool the hot embers with water, if available, or cover with lots of damp earth. This will stop any sparks from causing a bush fire.

## STAYING ALIVE: BUSH FIRE!

Bush fires are an unfortunate fact of life in Australia. Some can sweep across vast tracts of land, devastating plant and animal life. What should you do if you see flames?

**1. Water**. Get in a lake or large body of water, unless it is a fast-flowing and dangerous river.

**2. Tracks**. Head to a dirt track with no overhanging trees. A rocky plateau or gravel plain may offer you safety.

**3. Wind**. Be aware of the direction of the wind as this is where the bush fire is most likely to head.

**4. Run**. Don't try to outrun a bush fire directly—the fastest fires can outpace you. If you can see the main fire front clearly, run away and to the side of it.

**5. Heat**. Don't head uphill. Fires spread more quickly on an upslope because heat rises and causes vegetation farther uphill to catch alight.

# SEARCH AND RESCUE

A well-planned trip through the Australian outback involves letting others know your dates and route. When someone fails to return or reach their destination, it is taken seriously and search attempts are made quickly, from the ground and air.

If you're lucky, a plane will fly overhead. What can you use to make yourself more visible?

 ### Flying Doctors

Australia's Royal Flying Doctor Service flies throughout the outback providing vital medical help. In 2017, the service's 66 aircraft flew a total of 16,412,000 miles (26,412,555 km)—that's equal to 34 trips to the Moon and back. If you spot a plane, stand and wave your arms or a piece of bright clothing in a big arc above your head.

 ### Sticks and sand

Use a stick to scrawl a large message in sand. In 2015, after getting lost, 63-year-old Geoff Keys scrawled a giant "HELP 2807" message in a sandbank (the numbers stood for the day and month). He was soon rescued by helicopter.

 ### Thick smoke

If you are near an abandoned vehicle, consider burning rubber matting or the spare tire to send lots of thick, black smoke up into the air.

## Take the train

It's a long shot, but you may be near one of the trains that run through the outback. The Ghan runs from Adelaide to Darwin, cutting right through the center of Australia. The train may not be able to stop but if people see you, they may be able to phone or radio for help.

# REAL-LIFE SURVIVOR

A 41-year-old Dutch woman, Veronique Biunkens, got lost in the Australian outback for five days in 2016 but her survival skills got her through the ordeal. She covered her body in mud to act as a simple sunscreen and also made a shelter by dragging branches over two logs. At night, when the temperature dropped, she stuffed her clothing with tree moss to help keep her warm. You can achieve a similar effect with dry leaves and grasses, which help insulate you.

# CREATURE FEATURE:
## SOUTHERN CASSOWARY

With their large size and bright blue heads, you'll have no trouble identifying these 4–6-foot- (1.5–1.8-m-) tall flightless birds. They tend to be at their most aggressive when feeding and can kick with the long claws on their feet. They also peck with their beaks and attempt head-butts. Don't crouch if a bird threatens. Use your backpack or bag to shield your front as you back away, and shelter behind or even up a tree.

# MOVING ON

Moving might get you to a traffic-filled road, water hole, or a ranch in the distance. If it's hot, hot, hot, try to travel from very early morning until around 10:00 a.m., then seek shade, and only travel again when temperatures cool. If you have flashlights and plenty of batteries, consider traveling at night.

You'll need water, and plenty of it. But where in the outback are you going to get hold of the wet stuff?

## Animal tracks

A flock of birds may guide you to a billabong (a pool or backwater). Animal tracks all heading the same way may also lead you to water.

## Dried-up creeks

Small pools of water may exist in shaded areas of dried-up creeks or rivers. Or you can dig down 12–20 inches (30–50 cm) for water below the surface.

## Wells or water holes

Australian farms and ranches can be huge, so you may not see anyone, but you may come across cattle troughs, wells, or water holes for livestock. Fresh cow or sheep droppings may lead you to these.

## Mark your route

Leave messages and markers behind for rescuers to follow, such as arrows showing your direction of travel or tripods of sticks with something shiny on top to attract attention.

# REAL-LIFE SURVIVOR

In 2015, 62-year-old Reg Foggerdy got lost in the outback while on a hunting trip in Western Australia. Wearing only shorts, a t-shirt, and flip-flops—one of which he lost—he survived for six days, living off black ants. A search party was able to track his unusual foot and flip-flop tracks and rescued him.

## CREATURE FEATURE:
# SNAKES ALIVE!

Australia is home to many of the world's most venomous snakes. If you spot one, keep out of striking range and back away slowly. If bitten, try to keep the bite area at heart level, keep still, and slow your heart rate as much as possible.

**1. Inland taipan (right).** This shy and reclusive snake rarely attacks, which is just as well as it's one of the most venomous snakes in the world. A major bite can kill a person in under an hour.

**2. Common death adder (right).** Unlike most snakes, which slither away if a human approaches, the common death adder sits still and can strike the unwary.

**3. Eastern brown (right).** This bad-tempered snake slithers into an S shape with mouth wide open when threatening to strike. Its bite is fearsome as the venom can paralyze a victim.

# ADRIFT AT SEA

The five major oceans (the Pacific, Atlantic, Indian, Southern, and Arctic) cover 71 percent of the Earth's surface. Some parts, known as shipping lanes, are well-traveled by vessels carrying passengers and goods around the planet, but much of the remainder is isolated and under-explored. Finding yourself in the middle of an ocean can be terrifying, but remember, many people have survived such an ordeal.

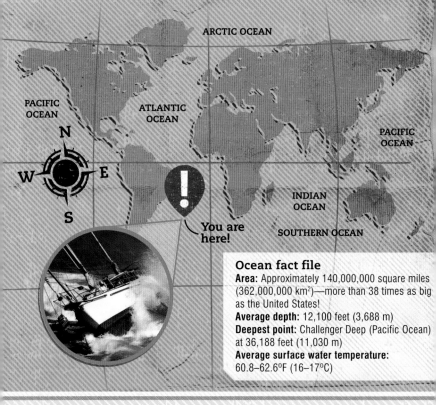

ARCTIC OCEAN

PACIFIC
OCEAN

ATLANTIC
OCEAN

PACIFIC
OCEAN

N

W        E

S

You are
here!

INDIAN
OCEAN

SOUTHERN OCEAN

### Ocean fact file
**Area:** Approximately 140,000,000 square miles (362,000,000 km²)—more than 38 times as big as the United States!
**Average depth:** 12,100 feet (3,688 m)
**Deepest point:** Challenger Deep (Pacific Ocean) at 36,188 feet (11,030 m)
**Average surface water temperature:** 60.8–62.6°F (16–17°C)

What event caused you to be cast adrift? You might have been cruising the coastline in a small boat which has been taken a long way out to sea. A handful of ocean survivors are victims of plane crashes or modern day pirates who steal your craft and leave you stranded in a lifeboat. You may have been on a ship that was wrecked during a storm, leaving you alone and far from shore.

## WHAT TO DO FIRST

Finding yourself alone at sea may present you with major challenges:

- Waves overturning your vessel
- Storms blowing you off course
- Exposure to extreme weather
- Lack of fresh water
- Heavy sea fog reducing visibility
- Icebergs in Southern and Arctic oceans
- Danger of running onto rocks
- Sharks and other dangerous marine animals

### Don't jump ship

If there is no risk of fire or sinking, don't abandon ship. You have more room, tools, and shelter than in a lifeboat. Rescuers are also more likely to spot you.

### Wear a life jacket

If you have to abandon ship and use a lifeboat, wear a life jacket and gather useful items, such as water and signaling devices, like flares.

### Assess your situation

Are you far from land? Do you have a working radio? Where are you? Consult charts or other navigation aids on board.

### Dress correctly

Make sure you are clothed as appropriately as possible for extreme weather conditions. If it's cold, warm layers of clothing and a woolly hat trap some warmth, even when wet.

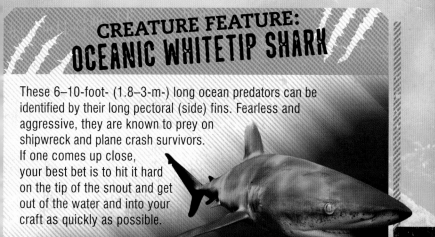

## CREATURE FEATURE:
## OCEANIC WHITETIP SHARK

These 6–10-foot- (1.8–3-m-) long ocean predators can be identified by their long pectoral (side) fins. Fearless and aggressive, they are known to prey on shipwreck and plane crash survivors. If one comes up close, your best bet is to hit it hard on the tip of the snout and get out of the water and into your craft as quickly as possible.

# IN THE WATER

Abandoning ship is a hard decision, but for some people, there's little choice. A fire may be raging on deck or your craft may be starting to tilt and sink. Before you exit, make sure you're wearing your life jacket and that all its straps are nice and tight.

Once the decision is made to leave your ship, get in a life raft. You may also find other items that can help you survive...

## Life rafts

Larger boats and all ships carry lifeboats or life rafts. These vary from small inflatable dinghies to fully-fledged boats. If you have a choice, go for the biggest —it may contain more supplies. Use rope to moor any spare life rafts together, just in case your craft develops a problem.

## Sea salvage

There might be plenty of items left floating in what is called the debris field. Scout the area for useful objects, such as buckets, water containers, ropes, more life jackets, plastic sheeting, tarpaulins, and pieces of wood with nails that can be used as fishing hooks.

## Ditch bag

Some vessels carry a bright orange, yellow or red "ditch bag" full of useful gear such as a first aid kit, food rations, knives, and water. Keep an eye out for one on board or floating in the water.

## EPIRBs

Short for Emergency Position Indicating Radio Beacons, these are tracking devices which give out a distress signal. They can be detected by satellites that relay the signals to the Coast Guard and emergency search and rescue bases.

Leaving a larger vessel usually means getting into a life raft. If disaster strikes, however, you may have to jump into the water.

**1. Reduce impact**. Jump from the lowest point of your craft to reduce impact with the water.

**2. Fold arms**. Fold your arms over your chest and grasp your life jacket with one hand and hold your nose with the other.

**3. Cross legs**. Leap away from the side of your ship and away from any stray cables. Cross your legs before entering the water. Use a doggy paddle stroke to swim to a nearby life raft or boat. This stroke may be slow but it is energy efficient so you won't tire as quickly as doing the front crawl.

## HELP yourself

The cold ocean water saps energy and cools you rapidly. If a rescue vessel is coming toward you but is some distance away, HELP yourself by adopting the heat escape lessening position (HELP). Fold your arms across your chest and cross your legs with your knees brought up toward your waist.

## Staying afloat

If you have no life jacket, try to stay afloat by alternating spells of treading water and breathing, then resting with your arms in front and your head just above the water.

# I'M OVER HERE!

Many stories of being lost at sea have a happy ending when survivors are spotted and rescued. That might mean being picked up by a passing ship. If someone knows a person is missing, there could be boats, planes, and helicopters out searching for them.

If you see the joyous sight of rescuers on the horizon, how do you make sure THEY see YOU? Start signaling! Here's how…

### Make a noise

Blowing a whistle as loudly as you can could help. Life rafts and life jackets often have a whistle attached.

### Get out your gear!

If you're in a life raft, it should have special gear, like a signaling kite, laser flashlights and flares, complete with instructions.

### Wave!

As the deep sea looks dark, wave something light or bright. One survivor was rescued after waving a surfboard at a helicopter crew. If you have nothing to wave, stick your arms out to your sides and wave them up and down slowly—a recognized distress signal.

### At night, flash a light

Life rafts and life jackets have flashlights, or you can use a normal flashlight or phone flashlight—if you have one. (Remember to keep it dry and don't use it until you need it, to save the batteries.)

# REAL-LIFE SURVIVOR

In 1942, during World War II, 25-year-old Poon Lim set sail from Cape Town, South Africa, on a merchant ship. Two days later, it was torpedoed by a German submarine and sank. Poon jumped into the sea and trod water, until he found one of the ship's life rafts. For the next 133 days, he drifted all the way across the Atlantic Ocean! He caught fish and seabirds to eat, and even managed to catch a shark and drink its blood because he was so thirsty. He was finally rescued by a fishing boat off the coast of Brazil.

## CREATURE FEATURE:
# DEADLY JELLIES

Poon Lim said he went swimming every day to keep fit, but it's a good idea to stay on board your boat or raft to avoid being stung by jellyfish! Here are some of the most dangerous…

**2. Lion's mane.** This huge, 6½-foot-(2-m-) wide jellyfish packs a nasty sting.

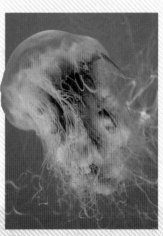

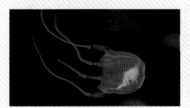

**1. Box jellyfish.** The world's deadliest jellyfish, its venom can kill in minutes.

**3. Portuguese man-of-war.** Not a true jellyfish, this stinging sea creature floats on the sea surface with its blue inflatable "sail."

# WATER EVERYWHERE

Water, water everywhere but none of it is drinkable! Do not drink sea water as it contains around 3.5 percent salt and will make you thirstier and more in need of fresh water than you were before. But do take advantage of any liquid found in canned food as well as rain that falls on you and your raft.

Aside from collecting rain water by any means possible, how can you protect yourself if left stranded in a boat or life raft?

### Take cover

Your raft may have a built-in canopy which keeps you in the shade and protects you from wind and rain. If not, use paddles or driftwood and plastic sheeting or tarpaulins to create cover.

### Keep cool

If it's hot, keep out of the sun as much as possible to reduce the risk of sunstroke, sunburn, and further dehydration. Cover your neck and head if you lack a wide-brimmed hat, and use a cloth soaked in seawater to cool yourself down.

### Stay dry

If it's cold, stay as dry as possible. Huddle in the bottom of your boat and cover yourself with tarpaulins, sails, or whatever you have handy.

### Find a container

Keep an empty food can, plastic cup, bucket, or other container to bail seawater out of your raft regularly. You may have to use it a lot if your boat springs a leak. Most inflatable life rafts come with repair patches, similar to fixing a bicycle tire puncture.

# STAYING ALIVE:
## COLLECTING WATER

Solar stills use the power of the sun to remove much of the salt from seawater. Some boats come with an inflatable floating version which you can tow behind you. Alternatively, you can make your own. Use a bucket or bowl, add seawater and a cup, and cover with a plastic sheet weighed down in the center by a small, heavy object, like a stone. The evaporated water condenses on the inside of the plastic sheet and drips down into the cup, leaving the salt behind in the bowl.

Plastic sheet

Small stone

Tape

Bowl

Cup

Seawater

# CREATURE FEATURE:
## FLYING SEA CREATURES

Some marine animals break the water's surface and launch themselves through the air, an action called breaching. While this can be amazing to watch, it can pose danger to you and your vessel.

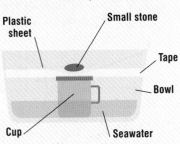

**Whales**. Gray and humpback whales, for example, can breach and crash into boats, damaging or destroying the craft. Even if one lands nearby, the impact of a whale on the water can cause your vessel to capsize.

**Rays**. There are over 600 species of rays, some of which, like the Manta ray, leap out of the water and can strike you or your craft.

# GOING THE DISTANCE

If you don't get rescued in the first few hours, you may have to sit tight and expect a long period at sea. If you've secured water supplies and are protected from the elements, then your next priority may be food.

So, if you're afloat at sea, stranded in a life raft in the middle of the ocean, where are you going to find food?

## Seaweed

Ocean seaweed is tough. Broader leafed species are less likely to make you ill. Wash it if you have large supplies of freshwater, otherwise dry it out in the sun.

## Emergency rations

Life rafts contain emergency rations and you may have salvaged other food from your stricken boat or ship. Try to make whatever you have last as long as possible.

## Fishing line

You can spear fish or snare seaweed with a fishing spear (see opposite). Alternatively, you can make a fishing line by attaching a bent pin or small nail to the end of a line. If you catch a fish, cut it, peel the skin, and slice the flesh into long strips, these can be dried in the sun. Don't eat the guts but use them as bait to catch more fish.

## Feeders

Small fish, shrimp, and crabs feed on seaweed, so if you pull some out of the sea, you may catch these too. Use a net, or pole and clothing to scoop the seaweed out.

## Simple spear

If you have bamboo, you can make a simple fishing spear.

**A.** Cut the bamboo lengthways to make four prongs about 6 inches (15 cm) long.

**B.** Wind string at the base of the cuts to keep the prongs apart.

**C.** Sharpen each prong to a point, giving you a four pronged spear.

# REAL-LIFE SURVIVORS

When Maurice and Maralyn Bailey's yacht sank after being struck by a whale, the pair took to their life raft. They survived an incredible 117 days in the Pacific Ocean before being rescued by a Korean fishing boat. The pair lived off their survival rations and caught fish and birds using safety pins bent into fishing hooks. They even caught baby sharks and sea turtles with their bare hands and ate them raw.

## CREATURE FEATURE:
## FEARSOME FISH

Some ocean fish can be too large or dangerous for you to handle. Two types of fish to be especially wary of are:

**1. Barracuda (above).** Slim but vicious fish whose pointed heads are packed with two sets of flesh-shredding teeth and a powerful jaw.

**2. Surgeonfish.** Also known as tangs, many species harbor a nasty weapon—venomous spines on either side of their tail.

# KEEP YOUR HOPES UP

One of the biggest trials facing a long-term sea survivor is mental not physical. With little to occupy you, long periods at sea can be distressing, but try to stay positive. Enjoy any surprises the sea brings, such as a piece of driftwood you can fashion into a paddle, and stay hopeful for rescue or a sight of land.

Stay alert: there are a number of signs, such as floating wood and vegetation, that may tell you land is nearby...

## Flocks of birds

Many birds head out to sea in flocks early in the day and return to roost on land at dusk. Note their flight direction; persistent bird cry from one direction in the evening may reveal their roosting place.

## Muddy water

Silty or muddy water when the sea is relatively calm is often the result of rivers and streams carrying sediment from the land out into the ocean.

## Cumulus cloud

A puffy cumulus cloud which doesn't appear to move when other clouds do can be a sign that an island lies below.

## Greenish glow

In tropical regions, the reflection of sunlight from shallow lagoons or coral reefs around an island can cause the sky to look greenish. You might also see the faint glow of a town at night.

# STAYING ALIVE:
## HEALTHY MIND AND BODY

If you are forced to spend days or even weeks on your own at sea, your mind can start to play tricks on you. How do you cope?

**1. Keep track**. Keep count of the days you are adrift by making a notch on a stick or some other mark for each day you're lost. Some sea survivors found that writing a daily journal helped them keep their focus.

**2. Calenture**. In tropical oceans, some people suffer from this type of heatstroke or fever. It can cause people to leap overboard, mistaking a stretch of sea ahead for green fields. Try to keep out of the sun and avoid dehydration.

# REAL-LIFE SURVIVORS

In 1972, the Robertson family from Scotland were sailing in the Pacific Ocean when their schooner yacht was damaged by a group of killer whales. The six people aboard, including Douglas (18) and twins Sandy and Neil (11) were all forced to abandon ship. They survived for 38 days in a small life raft and, when that sank, an even smaller 10-foot- (3-m-) long fiberglass dingy. They were finally rescued by a Japanese fishing trawler.

Enduring many storms, the six survivors collected rainwater to drink and also lived off sea turtles and small sharks which they caught with their bare hands or by a spear they made from a boat paddle. They drank the turtles' blood for extra moisture and used oils from their fat to treat body sores caused by constant exposure to salt water.

# GLOSSARY

**Antiseptic** substance which kills or prevents the growth and spread of harmful bacteria

**Avalanche** fast and sudden flow of snow down a slope

**Blizzard** severe snowstorms, usually accompanied by strong, high-speed winds

**Capsize** when a boat overturns in the water

**Condensation** drops of a liquid, usually water, that form when a gas cools and condenses

**Contaminate** when a substance becomes impure because something possibly dangerous has been added to it

**Dehydration** loss of water from something, such as a food or your body. Severe dehydration can be very harmful for the body.

**Downstream** point along a river or stream that is away from where you are, in the direction that the water is flowing

**Edible** something that can be eaten

**Evaporation** process of a liquid turning into a gas or vapor, such as water evaporating due to the heat of the Sun

**Fertile** area of land which is capable of growing and producing lots of plants

**Flares** devices used for signaling which, when activated, burn brightly

**Frostbite** injury to body tissue caused by extreme cold to parts of the body, such as the fingers, toes and nose

**GPS** short for global positioning system, this navigation system uses satellites orbiting Earth and is available on many smartphones

**Humidity** measure of the amount of water in the air. High humidity means the air contains a lot of water vapor.

**Hypothermia** dangerous physical condition in which body temperature drops below 95ºF (35ºC), affecting the brain and body, and sometimes leading to death

**Hydration** to absorb or take in water, such as when you take a drink

**Insulate** to cover or surround something to prevent heat from escaping

**Malaria** potentially life-threatening disease caused by a parasite carried by some mosquitoes, which can infect the human body through a mosquito bite

**Marooned** to be trapped and left alone in a hard-to-reach place, such as a desert island

**Oasis** place in a hot, dry desert where water and plants are found

**Paralyze** to lose the ability to move part or all of your body

**Plateau** area of mostly level, high ground

**Purify** to remove harmful or contaminating substances from something—often water

**Salvage** to recover items from a broken-down or wrecked vehicle, such as a car

**Solar still** device that uses the sun's energy to evaporate dirty water and then recollect it in a drinkable form

**Tinder** fine, small materials that can be lit to start a fire

**Toxic** something that is poisonous

**Venom** poison made by snakes, scorpions, and some other creatures, usually injected via biting or stinging